THE LATEST NINJA CREAMI COOKBOOK

1200 Days Ice Cream, Sorbet, Gelato, Milkshake, Smoothie Bowl and Ice Cream Mix-Ins Recipes To Master Your New Machine

NANNIE E. HORVATH

EDITOR: LYN   INTERIOR DESIGN: FAIZAN

COVER ART: ABR   FOOD STYLIST: JO

Table of Contents

Introduction

Say hello to the ultimate kitchen companion - the Ninja Creami. Designed with the health-conscious consumer in mind, the Ninja Creami lets you create delicious and healthy treats at home, without any of the guilt. With its advanced blending and freezing technology, the Ninja Creami makes it easy to whip up your own homemade ice creams, sorbets, and smoothies in a matter of minutes. And the best part? You can customize your creations with your favorite ingredients, and control the amount of sugar and fat in your treats. Whether you're looking to satisfy your sweet tooth, or simply want to enjoy a refreshing and nutritious snack, the Ninja Creami is the perfect tool for the job. So, why wait? Start creating your own frozen delights today with the Ninja Creami.

The Ninja Creami - a revolutionary kitchen appliance that will transform the way you make desserts and snacks at home. With its powerful blending capabilities and advanced freezing technology, the Ninja Creami can turn simple ingredients into creamy and delicious treats in just minutes. Whether you're looking to create healthy and nutritious snacks for your family or indulge in decadent desserts without the guilt, the Ninja Creami has got you covered. With its versatile features and ease of use, it's never been easier to whip up your own homemade ice creams, sorbets, smoothies, and more. Get ready to unleash your creativity and take your culinary skills to the next level with the Ninja Creami.

Chapter 1
Discover the Magic of the Ninja Creami

What is the Ninja Creami

The Ninja Creami is a kitchen appliance that allows you to make healthy and delicious frozen treats, such as ice cream, sorbet, and smoothies, at home. It is designed with advanced blending and freezing technology, and features a motorized base, a blending blade, and a freezer bowl. The Ninja Creami is versatile and easy to use, making it a great tool for anyone looking to create homemade treats without the added sugars and preservatives found in store-bought versions. It is also customizable, allowing you to create your own unique flavor combinations and adjust the amount of sugar and fat in your treats. With its ability to quickly and easily make a variety of different frozen treats, the Ninja Creami is an excellent addition to any kitchen.

How does it Work?

The Ninja Creami works by combining a motorized blending blade and a freezer bowl to create frozen treats in just minutes. The freezer bowl must first be placed in the freezer for a period of time to freeze. Once the bowl is frozen, it is placed onto the base of the Ninja Creami, and the blending blade is attached. The desired ingredients, such as fruits, nuts, or yogurt, are then added to the bowl, and the blade is turned on. As the blade spins, it chops and mixes the ingredients together, while the frozen walls of the bowl freeze the mixture. This creates a creamy and smooth texture, similar to traditional ice cream, sorbet, or smoothies.

The Ninja Creami is designed to be user-friendly, with easy-to-follow instructions for preparing and blending the ingredients. It is also customizable, allowing you to adjust the amount of sugar and fat in your treats to meet your personal preferences or dietary needs. The result is a healthy and delicious frozen treat that can be enjoyed anytime, without any of the preservatives or added sugars found in store-bought versions.

Benefits of Using the Ninja Creami In Your Kitchen

Healthy and Nutritious Treats: The Ninja Creami lets you create delicious and healthy frozen treats at home using fresh, natural ingredients. You can control the amount of sugar and fat in your treats, and choose healthier alternatives to traditional ice creams, such as dairy-free or low-sugar options.

Convenience: With the Ninja Creami, you can make frozen treats in just minutes, without the need for any special equipment or lengthy preparation. This makes it a great option for busy households or individuals who want a quick and easy dessert or snack.

Versatility: The Ninja Creami can make a variety of different frozen treats, including ice cream, sorbet, and smoothies. This means you can use it to create a range of different snacks and desserts, without needing to purchase multiple appliances.

Customization: The Ninja Creami is highly customizable, allowing you to create your own unique flavor combinations using your favorite ingredients. This means you can experiment with different flavors and textures to create treats that suit your personal tastes.

Cost-Effective: Making frozen treats at home using the Ninja Creami is often more cost-effective than buying store-bought versions. You can also reduce waste by using up leftover ingredients, which can save you money in the long run.

Fun and Engaging: Making frozen treats with the Ninja Creami can be a fun and engaging activity for families and individuals alike. It can be a great way to get kids involved in the kitchen and teach them about healthy eating.

Tips for Using and Cleaning the Ninja Creami

Freeze the bowl ahead of time: The Ninja Creami's freezer bowl needs to be frozen ahead of time, ideally for 24 hours, to ensure that it is completely frozen and ready to use.

Use fresh ingredients: To get the best results with the Ninja Creami, use fresh, high-quality ingredients. This will help ensure that your frozen treats have a great taste and texture.

Cut ingredients into small pieces: For best results, cut your ingredients into small pieces before adding them to the Ninja Creami. This will make it easier for the blender blade to mix them together and create a smooth and creamy texture.

Don't overfill the bowl: Be careful not to overfill the freezer bowl when adding ingredients. Leave some space at the top to allow the mixture to expand as it freezes.

Clean the blender blade carefully: The blender blade of the Ninja Creami can be sharp, so be careful when cleaning it. Use a soft sponge or cloth to clean the blade, and be sure to remove any stuck-on pieces of food.

Hand wash the bowl: The freezer bowl of the Ninja Creami should be hand-washed with warm, soapy water, and then dried thoroughly before being stored or used again.

Store the freezer bowl properly: When not in use, store the freezer bowl of the Ninja Creami in the freezer, so that it is always ready to use.

Q&As

Q: Can I make dairy-free or vegan ice cream with the Ninja Creami?

A: Absolutely! The Ninja Creami is perfect for making non-dairy or vegan ice cream using alternative milks like coconut, almond, or soy milk. You can also experiment with different sweeteners like agave, maple syrup, or honey to achieve the desired sweetness level. Just be sure to follow a recipe that is specifically designed for non-dairy or vegan ice cream, as the ingredient ratios and freezing times may be different than for traditional ice cream.

Q: Is it difficult to clean the Ninja Creami after making ice cream?

A: Not at all! The Ninja Creami is designed to be easy to clean, and most parts are dishwasher safe. To clean the blade and bowl, simply rinse them under warm water and use a soft sponge or brush to remove any leftover ice cream. The lid and other removable parts can be placed in the dishwasher for easy cleaning.

Q: Can I use fresh fruit in my ice cream base?

A: Yes, fresh fruit is a great addition to ice cream, sorbet, and other frozen treats. Just make sure to puree or chop it finely before adding it to the mix, as larger pieces can affect the texture of the final product. You can also experiment with different fruits, like berries, peaches, or mango, and combine them with other flavors like vanilla, chocolate, or coffee to create your own unique frozen dessert.

Q: How long does it take to make ice cream with the Ninja Creami?

A: The exact time will depend on the recipe and the temperature of your ingredients, but most ice cream recipes can be made in under 30 minutes. One of the benefits of the Ninja Creami is its powerful motor, which allows for quick and efficient blending and freezing of the ice cream base. Just be sure to follow the recipe carefully and monitor the consistency of the ice cream as it freezes.

Q: Can I make alcoholic frozen cocktails with the Ninja Creami?

A: Yes, the Ninja Creami is great for making frozen cocktails like margaritas or daiquiris. Just be sure to follow the recipe carefully and adjust the alcohol content as needed. Keep in mind that adding alcohol can affect the texture of the final product, so you may need to experiment with the ratio of alcohol to other ingredients to achieve the desired consistency. You can also try adding fresh fruit, herbs, or spices to create unique and flavorful frozen cocktails.

Chapter 2
Unleash the Power of the Ninja Creami

Choose Your Ingredients

Learn how to select the best ingredients for your ice cream and why it matters for texture and flavor. Selecting the best ingredients is key to making delicious ice cream with the perfect texture and flavor. Here are some tips for choosing the best ingredients for your ice cream:

1. Dairy: If you're making a traditional ice cream recipe, the quality of the dairy you use is crucial. Look for whole milk and heavy cream that is fresh and not overly processed. Avoid ultra-pasteurized products, as they can affect the texture of the ice cream.
2. Sweeteners: Choosing the right sweetener is important for achieving the desired sweetness level and texture. Granulated sugar is a common choice, but you can also use honey, maple syrup, agave, or other sweeteners. Be sure to dissolve your sweetener in your dairy mixture thoroughly to avoid any graininess.
3. Flavors: For the best flavor, use fresh and high-quality ingredients. If you're using fruit, choose ripe and flavorful varieties, and if you're using extracts, look for pure extracts rather than artificial ones.
4. Mix-ins: Adding mix-ins, such as nuts, candies, or fruits, can add texture and flavor to your ice cream. When adding mix-ins, be sure to chop them into small pieces, so they don't overwhelm the ice cream.

WHY IT MATTERS

Using high-quality and fresh ingredients can make a significant difference in the texture and flavor of your ice cream. For example, using fresh and ripe fruits can give your ice cream a more natural and vibrant flavor, while low-quality ingredients can affect the texture and make your ice cream grainy or icy. Choosing the right sweetener and using it correctly can also affect the texture and sweetness level of your ice cream. By selecting the best ingredients, you can create delicious and creamy ice cream that will leave your taste buds satisfied.

Types of Frozen Treats

The Ninja Creami can be used to make a variety of frozen treats, including:

1. Ice cream: This is the most common frozen dessert that can be made with the Ninja Creami. You can make traditional flavors like vanilla or chocolate, or get creative and experiment with new flavors like lavender honey or matcha green tea.
2. Gelato: Similar to ice cream, but with a richer and denser texture. Gelato is often made with a higher proportion of milk to cream and has less air churned into it during the freezing process.
3. Sorbet: A fruit-based frozen dessert that is typically dairy-free. Sorbet is refreshing and can be made with a

variety of fruits, such as strawberry, raspberry, or mango.

4. Frozen yogurt: A healthier alternative to ice cream that is made with yogurt instead of cream. Frozen yogurt is tangy and can be made with a variety of flavors and mix-ins, like fresh fruit or granola.
5. Sherbet: Similar to sorbet, but with a small amount of dairy added for a creamier texture. Sherbet is often made with citrus fruits, like orange or lime.
6. Frozen cocktails: With the Ninja Creami, you can also make frozen versions of your favorite cocktails, like margaritas or piña coladas.

EXAMPLES OF FLAVORS AND MIX-INS FOR EACH OF THESE FROZEN TREATS CAN INCLUDE:

•   Ice cream: classic vanilla, chocolate, strawberry, rocky road, mint chocolate chip, cookies and cream
•   Gelato: pistachio, hazelnut, tiramisu, salted caramel, dark chocolate
•   Sorbet: raspberry, lemon, pineapple, peach, blueberry
•   Frozen yogurt: vanilla bean, strawberry banana, honey Greek yogurt, chocolate fudge, pumpkin spice
•   Sherbet: orange, lime, raspberry, pineapple, lemon
•   Frozen cocktails: strawberry margarita, piña colada, frozen daiquiri, mojito, mudslide

With the Ninja Creami, the possibilities are endless, and you can create delicious and unique frozen treats to enjoy any time of the year.

Mix in Flavor

Incorporating your favorite flavors and add-ins into your ice cream base is a fun and creative way to make delicious, customized ice cream. Here are some tips and tricks for adding flavors and mix-ins to your ice cream base:

1. Infuse your base: Infusing your base with flavors can add depth and complexity to your ice cream. Heat your dairy and add any herbs or spices you want to infuse. Let it steep for about 30 minutes before straining it and adding it to your ice cream base.
2. Add extracts: Adding extracts, such as vanilla or almond, can add a subtle but delicious flavor to your ice cream. Use high-quality extracts, and add them sparingly until you achieve the desired flavor.
3. Use fresh fruit: Using fresh fruit in your ice cream can give it a natural and delicious flavor. Puree the fruit before adding it to your ice cream base, or chop it into small pieces for a chunky texture.
4. Add mix-ins: Adding mix-ins, such as chocolate chips or nuts, can add texture and flavor to your ice cream. Fold them into your ice cream base after it has churned for a few minutes, or layer them between scoops when storing your ice cream in the freezer.
5. Try savory flavors: Don't be afraid to experiment with savory flavors, such as bacon or herbs. These can add a unique twist to your ice cream and make it a memorable dessert.
6. Consider the texture: When adding mix-ins, consider the texture they will add to your ice cream. For example, adding chunks of frozen fruit can make your ice cream icy, while incorporating a sauce or puree can make it creamy and smooth.

By incorporating your favorite flavors and mix-ins into your ice cream base, you can create endless flavor combinations and have fun experimenting in the kitchen. Remember to be creative and have fun, and don't be afraid to try new flavor combinations!

Freeze Your Ice Cream

Properly freezing your ice cream is key to achieving the perfect texture and consistency. Here are some tips for freezing your ice cream using the Ninja Creami:

1. Set the temperature: Before you begin churning your ice cream, set your Ninja Creami to its coldest setting. This will ensure that your ice cream freezes quickly and evenly.
2. Chill the container: It's important to chill the container you'll be using to store your ice cream in the freezer. Place it in the freezer for at least 30 minutes before you begin churning your ice cream.
3. Churn your ice cream: Once your ice cream base is ready, pour it into the Ninja Creami and begin churning. Follow the manufacturer's instructions for churning time, which is typically between 15-30 minutes. As the ice cream churns, it will gradually thicken and become more creamy.
4. Transfer to the container: Once your ice cream has finished churning, quickly transfer it to the chilled container you prepared earlier. Use a spatula to scrape the ice cream out of the Ninja Creami, being careful not to overwork it.
5. Freeze the ice cream: Place the container of ice cream in the coldest part of your freezer and let it freeze for at least 4-6 hours, or until it is firm.

By following these steps, you can ensure that your ice cream freezes properly and has a smooth, creamy texture. It's important to note that the timing and temperature settings may vary depending on the recipe you're using and the specific model of Ninja Creami you have. Always refer to the manufacturer's instructions and use your own judgment to achieve the best results.

Serve and Store Your Ice Cream

Serving your ice cream in creative and fun ways can elevate your dessert experience and impress your guests. Here are some tips for serving your ice cream and storing it properly for later use:

1. Use fun toppings: Toppings can add texture and flavor to your ice cream, and are a great way to personalize each serving. Consider using sprinkles, nuts, chocolate chips, or fresh fruit as toppings.
2. Make ice cream sandwiches: Use cookies, waffles, or even donuts to sandwich your ice cream for a fun and indulgent dessert. You can also roll the edges in toppings for added texture and flavor.
3. Try an ice cream float: Pour your favorite soda or flavored sparkling water over a scoop of ice cream for a refreshing and bubbly dessert.
4. Store it properly: To keep your ice cream fresh and prevent freezer burn, store it in an airtight container in the coldest part of your freezer. Consider using a container with a tight-fitting lid, or cover it with plastic wrap before sealing it with the lid.
5. Thaw it properly: When you're ready to enjoy your ice cream, let it sit out at room temperature for a few minutes to soften. Avoid using the microwave to thaw your ice cream, as this can cause it to melt unevenly.
6. Experiment with flavors: Don't be afraid to experiment with different flavors and mix-ins. Consider trying seasonal flavors or adding unexpected ingredients, like spices or herbs, for a unique and memorable dessert.

The Ninja Creami is a powerful and versatile tool for creating delicious frozen treats right in your own kitchen. Whether you're a fan of traditional ice cream flavors or want to experiment with new and exciting combinations, the Ninja Creami makes it easy to achieve the perfect texture and flavor. With this cookbook as your guide, you'll be able to explore a wide range of frozen desserts and take your culinary creations to the next level. So, let's get started and unleash the full potential of the Ninja Creami!

Chapter 3
Ice Cream Recipes

Peaches And Cream Soft Serve Ice Cream

Prep time: 5 minutes | Cook time:35 Minutes | Serves 6

- 2 cups heavy cream
- 1 cup milk
- 3⁄4 cup sugar
- 1 Tbs. vanilla extract
- 1 cup sliced peaches

1. Refer to note at the beginning of the chapter about freezing bowl.
2. Puree the peaches in a food processor or blender.
3. Place the milk and cream in a bowl, and mix them together until well combined. Use a whisk to mix in the sugar. Continue to whisk for about 4 minutes until the sugar dissolves. Then mix in the vanilla extract. Then mix in the peaches.
4. Pour the ingredients into your ice cream maker, and let it churn for 25 minutes.
5. Serve immediately.

Orange Dream Soda Ice Cream

Prep time: 5 minutes | Cook time:2 Hours 50 Minutes | Serves 6

- 2 cups heavy cream
- 1 cup milk
- 3/4 cup sugar
- 1 teaspoon vanilla extract
- 20 ounces of your favorite orange soda

1. Refer to note at the beginning of the chapter about freezing bowl.
2. Place the milk and cream in a bowl, and mix them together until well combined. Use a whisk to mix in the sugar. Continue to whisk for about 4 minutes until the sugar dissolves. Then mix in the vanilla extract and orange soda.
3. Pour the ingredients into your ice cream maker, and let it churn for 25 minutes.
4. Put the ice cream in an airtight container and place in the freezer for around 2 hours. Allow the ice cream to thaw for 15 minutes before serving.

Low-sugar Vanilla Ice Cream

Prep time: 5 minutes | Cook time: 5 minutes | Serves 4

- 1¾ cup fat-free half-and-half
- ¼ cup stevia cane sugar blend
- 1 teaspoon vanilla extract

1. In a medium bowl, whisk the half-and-half, sugar, and vanilla together until everything is combined and the sugar is dissolved. The mixture will be foamy. Let it sit for 5 minutes or until the foam subsides.
2. Pour the base into a clean CREAMi Pint. Place the storage lid on the container and freeze for 24 hours.
3. Remove the CREAMi Pint from the freezer and take off the lid. Place the pint in the outer bowl of your Ninja CREAMi, install the Creamerizer Paddle in the outer bowl lid, and lock the lid assembly onto the outer bowl. Place the bowl assembly on the motor base, and twist the handle to the right to raise the platform and lock it in place. Select the Lite Ice Cream function.
4. Once the machine has finished processing, remove the ice cream from the pint. Serve immediately.

Almond Joy Soft Serve Ice Cream

Prep time: 5 minutes | Cook time: 35 minutes| Serves 6

- 2 cups heavy cream
- 1 cup milk
- 3⁄4 cup sugar
- 1 Tbs. vanilla extract
- 1 cup sliced Bananas
- 2 Almond Joy Candy Bars.

1. Refer to note at the beginning of the chapter about freezing bowl.
2. Place the milk & cream in a bowl. Mix together until well combined. Use a whisk to mix in the sugar. Continue to whisking 4 minutes until sugar dissolves. Then mix in the vanilla extract.
3. Place all the ingredients in a food processor or blender, and puree.
4. Pour ingredients into ice cream maker. Let it churn for 25 minutes.
5. Serve immediately.

Chocolate & Spinach Ice Cream

Prep time: 5 minutes | Cook time: 5 minutes | Serves 2

- ½ cup frozen spinach, thawed and squeezed dry
- 1 cup whole milk
- ½ cup granulated sugar
- 1 teaspoon mint extract
- 3-5 drops green food coloring
- ⅓ cup heavy cream
- ¼ cup chocolate chunks, chopped
- ¼ cup brownie, cut into 1-inch pieces

1. In a high-speed blender, add the spinach, milk, sugar, mint extract and food coloring and pulse until mixture smooth.
2. Transfer the mixture into an empty Ninja CREAMi pint container.
3. Add the heavy cream and stir until well combined.
4. Cover the container with the storage lid and freeze for 24 hours.
5. After 24 hours, remove the lid from container and arrange into the outer bowl of Ninja CREAMi.
6. Install the "Creamerizer Paddle" onto the lid of outer bowl.
7. Then rotate the lid clockwise to lock.
8. Press "Power" button to turn on the unit.
9. Then press "ICE CREAM" button.
10. When the program is completed, with a spoon, create a 1½-inch wide hole in the center that reaches the bottom of the pint container.
11. Add the chocolate chunks and brownie pieces into the hole and press "MIX-IN" button.
12. When the program is completed, turn the outer bowl and release it from the machine. 13. Transfer the ice cream into serving bowls and serve immediately.

Cinnamon Red Hot Ice Cream

Prep time: 5 minutes | Cook time: 10 minutes | Serves 5

- 2 cups heavy whipping cream, divided
- 1 egg yolk
- 1 cup half-and-half
- ½ cup Red Hot candies

1. In a mixing bowl, whisk together 1 cup of cream and the egg yolks until smooth.
2. In another large bowl, combine the half-and-half, 1 cup cream, and Red Hot candies. Whisk with a wooden spoon until the candies dissolve, about 5 to 10 minutes.
3. Pour the cream-egg mixture into the candy mixture and stir to incorporate.
4. Pour the mixture into an empty ninja CREAMi Pint container and freeze for 24 hours. 5. After 24 hours, remove the Pint from the freezer. Remove the lid.
5. Place the Ninja CREAMi Pint into the outer bowl. Place the outer bowl with the Pint in it into the ninja CREAMi machine and turn until the outer bowl locks into place. Push the ICE CREAM button.
6. Once the ICE CREAM function has ended, turn the outer bowl and release it from the ninja CREAMi machine.

Creamy Caramel Macchiato Coffee Ice Cream

Prep time: 5 minutes | Cook time: 5 minutes | Serves 6

- 1 cup heavy whipping cream
- ½ cup sweetened condensed milk
- ¼ cup coffee-mate caramel macchiato flavored creamer (liquid creamer)
- 1 teaspoon instant coffee granules
- Caramel syrup (for drizzling)

1. Combine all ingredients (except the syrup) in a big mixing bowl of a stand mixer or a large mixing dish.
2. Whip the heavy cream mixture with an electric mixer until firm peaks form (to prevent massive splattering, start at a slower speed, and as the cream thickens, increase the speed). Make sure the whip cream mixture isn't overmixed or "broken."
3. Pour the mixture into an empty ninja CREAMi Pint container and freeze for 24 hours. 4. After 24 hours, remove the Pint from the freezer. Remove the lid.
4. Place the Ninja CREAMi Pint into the outer bowl. Place the outer bowl with the Pint in it into the ninja CREAMi machine and turn until the outer bowl locks into place. Push the ICE CREAM button.
5. Once the ICE CREAM function has ended, turn the outer bowl and release it from the ninja CREAMi machine.

Spiced Ginger-peach Ice Cream Recipe

Prep time: 5 minutes | Cook time: 15 minutes| Serves 2

- 1 cup milk
- 3/4 cup white sugar
- 1/4 teaspoon salt
- 3 ounces peach puree
- 3/4 teaspoon ground ginger
- 1/2 teaspoon ground cinnamon , or more to taste
- 1/4 teaspoon vanilla extract
- 3 large eggs yolks egg yolks, lightly beaten
- 2 cups heavy whipping cream
- 4 small slice (blank)s fresh peach slices, diced, or more to taste

1. Whisk milk, sugar, and salt together in a saucepan over medium heat; bring to a simmer. Stir peach puree, ginger, cinnamon, and vanilla extract; simmer until flavors blend, 5 to 10 minutes.
2. Place egg yolks in a little bowl. Slowly pour 1/2 cup hot milk mixture into eggs, whisking constantly. Pour warmed egg mixture into the milk mixture in the saucepan over medium heat. Cook, stirring occasionally, until thick, 5 to ten minutes. Strain egg mixture right into a chilled bowl and refrigerate, stirring occasionally, until chilled, about 2 hours.
3. Whisk cream into chilled egg mixture; add peaches and stir.
4. Pour peach mixture in to the container of an ice cream maker and freeze according to the manufacturer's instructions.

Peanut Butter Ice Cream

Prep time: 5 minutes | Cook time: 5 minutes | Serves 4

- 1¾ cups skim milk
- 3 tablespoons smooth peanut butter
- ¼ cup stevia-cane sugar blend
- 1 teaspoon vanilla extract

1. In a bowl, add all ingredients and beat until smooth.
2. Set aside for about five minutes.
3. Transfer the mixture into an empty Ninja CREAMi pint container.
4. Cover the container with storage lid and freeze for 24 hours.
5. After 24 hours, remove the lid from container and arrange into the outer bowl of Ninja CREAMi.
6. Install the Creamerizer Paddle onto the lid of Outer Bowl.
7. Then rotate the lid clockwise to lock.
8. Press Power button to turn on the unit.
9. Then press Ice Cream button.
10. When the program is completed, turn the Outer Bowl and release it from the machine.
11. Transfer the ice cream into serving bowls and serve immediately.

Peanut Butter Banana Ice Cream Recipe

Prep time: 5 minutes | Cook time: 15 minutes| Serves 2

- 4 eaches ripe bananas, cut into 1-inch slices
- 1/4 cup peanut butter

1. Arrange banana slices on a baking sheet and freeze, 8 hours to overnight.
2. Process frozen bananas in a food processor until evenly chopped; add peanut butter and process until thick and creamy.

Coffee Ice Cream

Prep time: 5 minutes | Cook time: 5 minutes | Serves 4

- ¾ cup coconut cream
- ½ cup granulated sugar
- 1½ tablespoons instant coffee powder
- 1 cup rice milk
- 1 teaspoon vanilla extract

1. In a bowl, add coconut cream and beat until smooth.
2. Add the remaining ingredients and beat sugar is dissolved.
3. Transfer the mixture into an empty Ninja CREAMi pint container.
4. Cover the container with storage lid and freeze for 24 hours.
5. After 24 hours, remove the lid from container and arrange into the Outer Bowl of Ninja CREAMi.
6. Install the Creamerizer Paddle onto the lid of Outer Bowl.
7. Then rotate the lid clockwise to lock.
8. Press Power button to turn on the unit.
9. Then press Ice Cream button.
10. When the program is completed, turn the Outer Bowl and release it from the machine.
11. Transfer the ice cream into serving bowls and serve immediately.

Mounds Soft Serve Ice Cream

Prep time: 5 minutes | Cook time: 35 minutes| Serves 6

- 2 cups heavy cream
- 1 cup milk
- 3⁄4 cup sugar
- 1 Tbs. vanilla extract
- 1 cup sliced Bananas
- 2 Mounds Candy Bars.

1. Refer to note at the beginning of the chapter about freezing bowl.
2. Place the milk & cream in a bowl. Mix together until well combined. Use a whisk to mix in the sugar. Continue to whisking 4 minutes until sugar dissolves. Then mix in the vanilla extract.
3. Place all the ingredients in a food processor or blender, and puree.
4. Pour ingredients into ice cream maker. Let it churn for 25 minutes.

Classic Vanilla Ice Cream

Prep time: 5 minutes | Cook time: 5 minutes | Serves 4

- 1 tablespoon cream cheese, at room temperature
- 1⁄3 cup granulated sugar
- 1 teaspoon vanilla extract
- 3⁄4 cup heavy (whipping) cream
- 1 cup whole milk
- 1⁄4 cup mini chocolate chips (optional)

1. In a large microwave-safe bowl, add the cream cheese and microwave for 10 seconds. Add the sugar and vanilla extract, and with a whisk or rubber spatula, combine the mixture until it looks like frosting, about 60 seconds.
2. Slowly whisk in the heavy cream and milk and mix until the sugar is completely dissolved and the cream cheese is completely incorporated.
3. Pour the base into a clean CREAMi Pint. Place the storage lid on the container and freeze for 24 hours.
4. Remove the CREAMi Pint from the freezer and take off the lid. Place the pint container in the outer bowl of your Ninja CREAMi, install the Creamerizer Paddle in the outer bowl lid, and lock the lid assembly onto the outer bowl. Place the bowl assembly on the motor base, and twist the handle to the right to raise the platform and lock it in place. Select the Ice Cream function.
5. Once the machine has finished processing, remove the lid from the pint container. If you are adding chocolate chips: with a spoon, create a 1½-inch-wide hole that reaches the bottom of the pint. During this process, it is okay if your treat reaches above the Max Fill line. Add ¼ cup of mini chocolate chips to the hole in the pint, replace the lid, and select the Mix-In function.
6. Serve immediately with desired toppings.

Baby Ruth Soft Serve Ice Cream
Prep time: 5 minutes | Cook time: 35 minutes| Serves 6

- 2 cups heavy cream
- 1 cup milk
- 3⁄4 cup sugar
- 1 Tbs. vanilla extract
- 1 cup sliced Bananas
- 2 Baby Ruth Candy Bars.

1. Refer to note at the beginning of the chapter about freezing bowl.
2. Place the milk & cream in a bowl. Mix together until well combined. Use a whisk to mix in the sugar. Continue to whisking 4 minutes until sugar dissolves. Then mix in the vanilla extract.
3. Place all the ingredients in a food processor or blender, and puree.
4. Pour ingredients into ice cream maker. Let it churn for 25 minutes.
5. Serve immediately.

Vegan Chocolate Soft Serve Ice Cream
Prep time: 5 minutes | Cook time:50 Minutes | Serves 9

- 3/4 cup water
- 1 1/4 cups full fat coconut milk or coconut cream (as thick as possible)
- 2/3 cup organic cane sugar
- 2/3 cup unsweetened cocoa powder
- 1/4 tsp sea salt
- 6 ounces vegan dark chocolate, finely chopped
- 1/2 tsp pure vanilla extract

1. Refer to note at the beginning of the chapter about freezing bowl.
2. Put the first 5 ingredients in a large saucepan, and heat it on medium-high heat. Mix the ingredients together using a whisk. Allow the mixture to come to a low boil. Continue to whisk often, and remain cooking on a low boil for 1 minute.
3. Take the pan off the heat, and mix in the chocolate and vanilla extract using the whisk. Continue to mix until the chocolate is melted.
4. Place the mixture in a blender, and blend on high speed for about 30 seconds.
5. Allow the mixture to cool
6. Pour the ingredients into your ice cream maker, and let it churn for 25 minutes.
7. Serve immediately.

Zero Soft Serve Ice Cream
Prep time: 5 minutes | Cook time: 35 minutes| Serves 4

- 2 cups heavy cream
- 1 cup milk
- 3⁄4 cup sugar
- 1 Tbs. vanilla extract
- 1 cup sliced Bananas
- 2 Zero Candy Bars.

1. Refer to note at the beginning of the chapter about freezing bowl.
2. Place the milk & cream in a bowl. Mix together until well combined. Use a whisk to mix in the sugar. Continue to whisking 4 minutes until sugar dissolves. Then mix in the vanilla extract.
3. Place all the ingredients in a food processor or blender, and puree.
4. Pour ingredients into ice cream maker. Let it churn for 25 minutes.

Milky Way Soft Serve Ice Cream
Prep time: 5 minutes | Cook time: 35 minutes| Serves 4

- 2 cups heavy cream
- 1 cup milk
- 3⁄4 cup sugar
- 1 Tbs. vanilla extract
- 1 cup sliced Bananas
- 2 Milky Way Candy Bars.

1. Refer to note at the beginning of the chapter about freezing bowl.
2. Place the milk & cream in a bowl. Mix together until well combined. Use a whisk to mix in the sugar. Continue to whisking 4 minutes until sugar dissolves. Then mix in the vanilla extract.
3. Place all the ingredients in a food processor or blender, and puree.
4. Pour ingredients into ice cream maker. Let it churn for 25 minutes.

Butterfinger Soft Serve Ice Cream

Prep time: 5 minutes | Cook time: 35 minutes| Serves 6

- 2 cups heavy cream
- 1 cup milk
- 3⁄4 cup sugar
- 1 Tbs. vanilla extract
- 1 cup sliced Bananas
- 2 Butterfinger Candy Bars.

1. Refer to note at the beginning of the chapter about freezing bowl.
2. Place the milk & cream in a bowl. Mix together until well combined. Use a whisk to mix in the sugar. Continue to whisking 4 minutes until sugar dissolves. Then mix in the vanilla extract.
3. Place all the ingredients in a food processor or blender, and puree.
4. Pour ingredients into ice cream maker. Let it churn for 25 minutes.
5. Serve immediately.

Maple Walnut Ice Cream Recipe

Prep time: 5 minutes | Cook time: 15 minutes| Serves 2

- 1 1/2 cups heavy whipping cream
- 5 large eggs yolks egg yolks
- 1 1/2 cups milk
- 2 tablespoons white sugar
- 1 tablespoon corn syrup
- 3/4 cup maple syrup
- 1 teaspooncoarse salt
- 1/4 teaspoon vanilla extract
- 1 1/2 cups walnut halves
- 1/2 cup maple syrup
- 1 tablespoon maple syrup
- 1 pinch salt

1. Pour cream into a large bowl and set a mesh strainer over the bowl. Whisk egg yolks together in a separate bowl.
2. Heat milk, sugar, and corn syrup together in a saucepan over medium-low heat until milk begins to steam, about 5 minutes. Slowly pour about 1/2 cup heated milk into the egg yolks, whisking constantly. Scrape egg yolk mixture into the saucepan with a heatproof spatula.
3. Cook and stir milk mixture constantly with the spatula, scraping the bottom of the saucepan often, until mixture thickens and coats the spatula, about 10 minutes. Remove saucepan from heat; pour mixture through the mesh strainer into the cream.
4. Stir 3/4 cup maple syrup, coarse salt, and vanilla into cream mixture, then place the bowl over a larger bowl of ice water; stir to cool to room temperature. Chill mixture in the refrigerator, about 2 hours.
5. Preheat oven to 275 degrees F (135 degrees C). Spread walnuts onto a baking sheet.
6. Toast walnuts in the preheated oven until they turn golden brown and become fragrant, about 15 minutes. Set nuts aside to cool to room temperature. Chop nuts coarsely.
7. Heat the 1/2 cup plus 1 tablespoon maple syrup in a saucepan until it comes to a boil. Stir in walnuts, and return to a boil. Stir nuts for 10 seconds, remove from heat; set aside to cool completely. The nuts will be wet and sticky when cooled.
8. Remove cream mixture from the refrigerator, pour into your ice cream maker, and freeze according to manufacturer's instructions. During the last few minutes of churning, stir in wet walnuts.

Fast And Easy Creamy Ice Cream Recipe

Prep time: 5 minutes | Cook time: 15 minutes| Serves 2

- 1 quart half-and-half
- 1 (3.5 ounce) package instant pudding mix, any flavor

1. Place the bowl of an ice cream maker in the freezer until completely chilled, at least one hour.
2. Chill half-and-half in the freezer, shaking every ten minutes, until chilled but not frozen, about 30 minutes.
3. Pour chilled half-and-half and pudding mix right into a bowl and mix well with a whisk.
4. Place frozen plate of ice cream maker into the ice cream maker; add the stirring component and lid. Turn on the machine so the bowl is rotating. Pour pudding mixture into the machine through the hole in the lid.
5. Allow ice cream to process in the ice cream maker until desired consistency is reached, about 30 minutes.

Creamy Lemon Grass Ice Cream Recipe

Prep time: 5 minutes | Cook time: 15 minutes| Serves 2

- 2 cups light cream
- 1 1/2 cups fat free sweetened condensed milk
- 3 stalks chopped lemons grass
- 2 large eggs yolks egg yolks

1. Heat cream, condensed milk, lemon grass in a saucepan over medium heat until mixture steams. Remove from heat prior to the mixture boils and invite to steep for at least 30 minutes, up to 1 one hour and 30 minutes.
2. Reheat the cream mixture over medium heat until it begins to steam. Whisk egg yolks in a little bowl. Temper the egg yolks by pouring a little amount of the hot mixture in while whisking constantly in order to avoid scrambling the eggs.
3. Pour the warm egg mixture into the cream mixture. Continue steadily to cook and stir before mixture has the capacity to coat the back of a spoon. Strain mixture through a sieve to eliminate the bits of lemon grass. Refrigerate until cold.
4. Pour the chilled mixture into an ice cream maker and freeze according to manufacturer's directions until it reaches "soft-serve" consistency. Transfer ice cream to a one- or two-quart lidded plastic container; cover surface with plastic wrap and seal. For best results, ice cream should ripen in the freezer for at least 2 hours or overnight.

Peanut Butter-banana V'ice Cream

Prep time: 5 minutes | Cook time: 15 minutes| Serves 2

- 4 very ripe bananas
- 1/4 cup peanut butter (smooth or chunky)
- 1 tablespoon coconut oils
- 1/2 teaspoon ground cinnamon
- 1/4 teaspoon grated nutmeg
- pinch of kosher salt

1. Slice bananas into 1/4"-thick rounds and devote a ziptop plastic bag. Lay the slices flat in a single layer in the freezer therefore the rounds freeze individually rather than in a large clump.
2. Freeze the bananas for at least 2 hours and up to overnight. Place the frozen bananas, peanut butter, coconut oil, cinnamon, nutmeg, and salt in a food processor or blender and let sit for 2 or 3 three minutes. Then puree until creamy and smooth. If you like a frozen yogurt consistency, then serve it up.
3. If you like a firmer ice cream experience, spoon it right into a container and freeze for approximately an hour.

Snow Cream Recipe

Prep time: 5 minutes | Cook time: 15 minutes| Serves 2

- 8 cups clean fresh snow
- 1 (14-ounce) can sweetened condensed milk
- 1 tablespoon vanilla extract

1. Mix snow, sweetened condensed milk, and vanilla extract together in a bowl until well mixed.

Easy Snow Ice Cream Recipe

Prep time: 5 minutes | Cook time: 15 minutes| Serves 2

- 1 (14-ounce) can sweetened condensed milk
- 3/4 cup white sugar
- 1 1/2 teaspoons vanilla extract
- 1 gallon clean fresh snow

1. Stir sweetened condensed milk, sugar, and vanilla extract together in a huge bowl until smooth.
2. Gradually stir snow into milk mixture until your desired consistency is reached.

Chapter 4
Gelato & Sorbet Recipes

Caribbean Pineapple Sorbet

Prep time: 5 minutes | Cook time:2 Hours 40 Minutes | Serves 9

- 1 diced, peeled, and cored small pineapple
- 2 tablespoons lemon juice
- 1 cup plus 2 tablespoons sugar

1. Refer to note at the beginning of the chapter about freezing bowl.
2. Puree the pineapple and lemon juice in a food processor or blender. Then add in the sugar and puree until the sugar dissolves.
3. Pour the ingredients into your ice cream maker, and let it churn for 25-30 minutes.
4. Place in an airtight container for up to 2 hours, until desired consistency is reached.

Mango Madness Coconut Raspberry Sorbet

Prep time: 5 minutes | Cook time:5 Hours 35 Minutes | Serves 11

- 3 cups packed, cubed mango
- 1 cup fresh raspberries
- 1 cup full-fat coconut milk
- 1 cup sugar
- Pinch of salt
- 1 teaspoon lime juice

1. Refer to note at the beginning of the chapter about freezing bowl.
2. Puree all the ingredients in a food processor or blender. Then transfer the mixture to a bowl, and refrigerate covered for 3-4 hours.
3. Pour the ingredients into your ice cream maker, and let it churn for 25-30 minutes.
4. Place in an airtight container for up to 2 hours, until desired consistency is reached.

Double Dark Chocolate Gelato

- 12 cup heavy cream
- 2 cups milk
- 34 cup sugar
- 14 teaspoon salt
- 7 ounces high quality dark chocolate
- 1 teaspoon vanilla extract

1. Melt the chocolate, and allow it to cool a little bit.
2. Place the milk and cream in a bowl, and mix them together until well combined. Use a whisk to mix in the sugar and salt. Continue to whisk for about 4 minutes until the sugar and salt dissolve. Then mix in the vanilla extract. Finally mix in the chocolate until well combined.
3. Pour the ingredients into your ice cream maker, and let it churn for 25 minutes.
4. Put the gelato in an airtight container and place in the freezer for up to 2 hours, until desired consistency is reached.

Tropical Watermelon Lemon/lime Sorbet

Prep time: 5 minutes | Cook time:2 Hours 40 Minutes | Serves 6

- 3 1/2 cups sliced seedless watermelon
- 6-ounce chilled pineapple juice
- 3/4 cup chilled ginger ale
- ½ cup fresh lime juice
- 1/3 cup grenadine

1. Puree all ingredients in a food processor or blender.
2. Pour the ingredients into your ice cream maker, and let it churn for 25-30 minutes.
3. Place in an airtight container for up to 2 hours, until desired consistency is reached.

Honey Peach Gelato

- 1/2 cup heavy cream
- 2 cups milk
- 3/4 cup sugar
- 1 cup sliced peaches
- 1 tablespoon vanilla extract
- 1/4 cup honey

1. Puree the peaches in a food processor or blender.
2. Place the milk and cream in a bowl, and mix them together until well combined. Use a whisk to mix in the sugar. Continue to whisk for about 4 minutes until the sugar dissolves. Then mix in the vanilla extract honey and peach puree.
3. Pour the ingredients into your ice cream maker, and let it churn for 25 minutes.
4. Put the gelato in an airtight container and place in the freezer for up to 2 hours, until desired consistency is reached.

Tiramisu Gelato

Prep time: 15 minutes | Cook time: 6 minutes | Serves 4

- 4 large egg yolks
- ⅓ cup granulated sugar
- 1 cup whole milk
- ⅓ cup heavy (whipping) cream
- ¼ cup cream cheese
- 1 tablespoon instant coffee
- 1 teaspoon rum extract
- ¼ cup ladyfinger pieces

1. Fill a large bowl with ice water and set it aside.
2. In a small saucepan, whisk together the egg yolks and sugar until the mixture is fully combined and the sugar is dissolved. Do not do this over heat.
3. Whisk in the milk, heavy cream, cream cheese, instant coffee, and rum extract.
4. Place the pan over medium heat. Cook, stirring constantly with a rubber spatula, until the temperature reaches 165°F to 175°F on an instant-read thermometer.
5. Remove the pan from the heat and pour the base through a fine-mesh strainer into a clean CREAMi Pint. Carefully place the container in the prepared ice water bath, making sure the water doesn't spill into the base.
6. Once the base has cooled, place the storage lid on the pint and freeze for 24 hours.
7. Remove the pint from the freezer and take off the lid. Place the pint in the outer bowl of your Ninja CREAMi, install the Creamerizer Paddle in the outer bowl lid, and lock the lid assembly onto the outer bowl. Place the bowl assembly on the motor base, and twist the handle to the right to raise the platform and lock it in place. Select the Gelato function.
8. Once the machine has finished processing, remove the lid from the pint container. With a spoon, create a 1½-inch-wide hole that reaches the bottom of the pint. During this process, it is okay if your treat reaches above the Max Fill line. Add the ladyfinger pieces to the hole in the pint, replace the lid, and select the Mix-In function.
9. Once the machine has finished processing, remove the gelato from the pint. Serve immediately.

Lime Beer Sorbet

Prep time: 5 minutes | Cook time: 5 minutes | Serves 4

- ¾ cup beer
- ⅔ cup water
- ½ cup fresh lime juice
- ¼ cup granulated sugar

1. In a high-speed blender, add all the ingredients and pulse until smooth.
2. Set aside for about 5 minutes.
3. Transfer the mixture into an empty Ninja CREAMi pint container.
4. Cover the container with the storage lid and freeze for 24 hours.
5. After 24 hours, remove the lid from container and arrange into the outer bowl of Ninja CREAMi.
6. Install the "Creamerizer Paddle" onto the lid of outer bowl.
7. Then rotate the lid clockwise to lock.
8. Press "Power" button to turn on the unit.
9. Then press "SORBET" button.
10. When the program is completed, turn the outer bowl and release it from the machine 11. Transfer the sorbet into serving bowls and serve immediately.

Mango Sorbet

Prep time: 5 minutes | Cook time: 5 minutes | Serves 4

- 4 cups mangoes, peeled, pitted and chopped
- ½ cup water
- ⅓-½ cup sugar
- ¼ cup fresh lime juice
- 2 tablespoons Chamoy

1. In a high-speed blender, add mangoes and water and pulse until smooth.
2. Through a fine-mesh strainer, strain the mango puree into a large bowl.
3. Add the sugar, lime juice and chamoy and stir to combine.
4. Transfer the mixture into an empty Ninja CREAMi pint container.
5. Cover the container with storage lid and freeze for 24 hours.
6. After 24 hours, remove the lid from container and arrange into the Outer Bowl of Ninja CREAMi.
7. Install the Creamerizer Paddle onto the lid of Outer Bowl.
8. Then rotate the lid clockwise to lock.
9. Press Power button to turn on the unit.
10. Then press Sorbet button.
11. When the program is completed, turn the Outer Bowl and release it from the machine.
12. Transfer the sorbet into serving bowls and serve immediately.

Plum Sorbet

Prep time: 5 minutes | Cook time: 5 minutes | Serves 4

- 1 can plums

1. Place the plums into an empty Ninja CREAMi pint container.
2. Cover the container with storage lid and freeze for 24 hours.
3. After 24 hours, remove the lid from container and arrange into the Outer Bowl of Ninja CREAMi.
4. Install the Creamerizer Paddle onto the lid of Outer Bowl.
5. Then rotate the lid clockwise to lock.
6. Press Power button to turn on the unit.
7. Then press Sorbet button.
8. When the program is completed, turn the Outer Bowl and release it from the machine. 9. Transfer the sorbet into serving bowls and serve immediately.

Cherry-berry Rosé Sorbet

Prep time: 5 minutes | Cook time: 10 minutes | Serves 3

- 2 cups frozen cherry-berry fruit blend
- ½ cup rosé wine, or as needed
- ¼ cup white sugar, or to taste
- ¼ medium lemon, juiced

1. Add all ingredients to a bowl and mix until the sugar dissolves. Place the mixture in the ninja CREAMi Pint container and freeze on a level surface in a cold freezer for a full 24 hours.
2. After 24 hours, remove the Pint from the freezer. Remove the lid.
3. Place the Ninja CREAMi Pint into the outer bowl. Place the outer bowl with the Pint in it into the ninja CREAMi machine and turn until the outer bowl locks into place. Push the SORBET button. During the SORBET function, the sorbet will mix together and become very creamy. This should take approximately 2 minutes.
4. Once the SORBET function has ended, turn the outer bowl and release it from the ninja CREAMi machine.
5. Your sorbet is ready to eat! Enjoy!

Pineapple & Rum Sorbet

Prep time: 5 minutes | Cook time: 5 minutes | Serves 4

- ¾ cup piña colada mix
- ¼ cup rum
- 2 tablespoons granulated sugar
- 1½ cups frozen pineapple chunks

1. In a high-speed blender, add all the ingredients and pulse until smooth.
2. Transfer the mixture into an empty Ninja CREAMi pint container.
3. Cover the container with storage lid and freeze for 24 hours.
4. After 24 hours, remove the lid from container and arrange into the Outer Bowl of Ninja CREAMi.
5. Install the Creamerizer Paddle onto the lid of Outer Bowl.
6. Then rotate the lid clockwise to lock.
7. Press Power button to turn on the unit.
8. Then press Sorbet button.
9. When the program is completed, turn the Outer Bowl and release it from the machine. 10. Transfer the sorbet into serving bowls and serve immediately.

Lemony Herb Sorbet

Prep time: 5 minutes | Cook time: 6 minutes | Serves 4

- ½ cup water
- ¼ cup granulated sugar
- 2 large fresh dill sprigs, stemmed
- 2 large fresh basil sprigs, stemmed
- 1 cup ice water
- 2 tablespoons fresh lemon juice

1. In a small saucepan, add sugar and water and over medium heat and cook for about five minutes or until the sugar is dissolved, stirring continuously.
2. Stir in the herb sprigs and remove from the heat.
3. Add the ice water and lemon juice and stir to combine.
4. Transfer the mixture into an empty Ninja CREAMi pint container.
5. Cover the container with storage lid and freeze for 24 hours.
6. After 24 hours, remove the lid from container and arrange into the Outer Bowl of Ninja CREAMi.
7. Install the Creamerizer Paddle onto the lid of Outer Bowl.
8. Then rotate the lid clockwise to lock.
9. Press Power button to turn on the unit.
10. Then press Sorbet button.
11. When the program is completed, turn the Outer Bowl and release it from the machine.
12. Transfer the sorbet into serving bowls and serve immediately.

Peach Sorbet

Prep time: 5 minutes | Cook time: 5 minutes | Serves 4

- 1 cup passionfruit seltzer
- 3 tablespoons agave nectar
- 1 can peaches in heavy syrup, drained

1. In a bowl, add the seltzer and agave and beat until agave is dissolved.
2. Place the peaches into an empty Ninja CREAMi pint container and top with seltzer mixture.
3. Cover the container with storage lid and freeze for 24 hours.
4. After 24 hours, remove the lid from container and arrange into the Outer Bowl of Ninja CREAMi.
5. Install the Creamerizer Paddle onto the lid of Outer Bowl.
6. Then rotate the lid clockwise to lock.
7. Press Power button to turn on the unit.
8. Then press Sorbet button.
9. When the program is completed, turn the Outer Bowl and release it from the machine. 10. Transfer the sorbet into serving bowls and serve immediately.

Mango Chamoy Sorbet

Prep time: 5 minutes | Cook time: 5 minutes | Serves 4

- 4 cups mangoes, peeled, pitted and chopped
- ½ cup water
- ⅓-½ cup sugar
- ¼ cup fresh lime juice
- 2 tablespoons chamoy

1. In a high-speed blender, add mangoes and water and pulse until smooth.
2. Through a fine-mesh strainer, strain the mango puree into a large bowl.
3. Add the sugar, lime juice and chamoy and stir to combine.
4. Transfer the mixture into an empty Ninja CREAMi pint container.
5. Cover the container with the storage lid and freeze for 24 hours.
6. After 24 hours, remove the lid from container and arrange into the outer bowl of Ninja CREAMi.
7. Install the "Creamerizer Paddle" onto the lid of outer bowl.
8. Then rotate the lid clockwise to lock.
9. Press "Power" button to turn on the unit.
10. Then press "SORBET" button.
11. When the program is completed, turn the outer bowl and release it from the machine. 12. Transfer the sorbet into serving bowls and serve immediately.

Chocolate Cauliflower Gelato

Prep time: 15 minutes | Cook time: 3 minutes | Serves 4

- 1 cup whole milk
- ½ cup heavy cream
- ⅓ cup sugar
- 2 tablespoons cocoa powder
- ½ cup frozen cauliflower rice
- ¼ teaspoon almond extract
- Pinch of salt
- ½ cup dark chocolate, chopped

1. In a small saucepan, add all ingredients except for chopped chocolate and beat until well combined.
2. Place the saucepan over medium heat and cook for about 2-3 minutes, stirring continuously.
3. Remove from the heat and transfer the mixture into an empty Ninja CREAMi pint container.
4. Place the container into an ice bath to cool.
5. After cooling, cover the container with the storage lid and freeze for 24 hours.
6. After 24 hours, remove the lid from container and arrange into the outer bowl of Ninja CREAMi.
7. Install the "Creamerizer Paddle" onto the lid of outer bowl.
8. Then rotate the lid clockwise to lock.
9. Press "Power" button to turn on the unit.
10. Then press "GELATO" button.
11. When the program is completed, with a spoon, create a 1½-inch wide hole in the center that reaches the bottom of the pint container.
12. Add the chopped chocolate into the hole and press "MIX-IN" button.
13. When the program is completed, turn the outer bowl and release it from the machine. 14. Transfer the gelato into serving bowls and serve immediately.

Blueberry Lemon Sorbet

Prep time: 5 minutes | Cook time: 5 minutes | Serves 1

- 1 tablespoon cream cheese
- ¼ cup milk
- 1½ cups lemonade
- ⅓ cup blueberries (fresh or frozen)

1. In a medium mixing bowl, whisk together the softened cream cheese and the milk. Make an effort to integrate the two as much as possible. Some little bits of cream cheese may remain, but that's fine as long as they're small.
2. Add the lemonade and stir thoroughly.
3. Pour the mixture into a ninja CREAMi Pint container, add the blueberries and freeze on a level surface in a cold freezer for a full 24 hours.
4. After 24 hours, remove the Pint from the freezer. Remove the lid.
5. Place the Ninja CREAMi Pint into the outer bowl. Place the outer bowl with the Pint in it into the ninja CREAMi machine and turn until the outer bowl locks into place. Push the SORBET button. During the SORBET function, the sorbet will mix together and become very creamy. This should take approximately 2 minutes.
6. Once the SORBET function has ended, turn the outer bowl and release it from the ninja CREAMi machine.
7. Your sorbet is ready to eat! Enjoy!
8. Place the outer bowl with the Pint back into the ninja CREAMi machine and lock it into place if the sorbet isn't quite creamy enough. Select the RE-SPIN option. Remove the outer bowl from the Ninja CREAMi after the RE-SPIN cycle is complete.

Coconut Lime Sorbet

Prep time: 5 minutes | Cook time: 30 minutes | Serves 5

- 1 can coconut cream
- ½ cup coconut water
- ¼ cup lime juice
- ½ tablespoon lime zest
- ¼ teaspoon coconut extract (optional)

1. Combine the coconut cream, coconut water, lime juice, lime zest, and coconut extract in a mixing bowl. Cover with plastic wrap and refrigerate for at least 1 hour, or until the flavors have melded.
2. Add the mixture to the Ninja CREAMi Pint container and freeze on a level surface in a cold freezer for a full 24 hours.
3. After 24 hours, remove the Pint from the freezer. Remove the lid.
4. Place the Ninja CREAMi Pint into the outer bowl. Place the outer bowl with the Pint in it into the ninja CREAMi machine and turn until the outer bowl locks into place. Push the SORBET button. During the SORBET function, the sorbet will mix together and become very creamy. This should take approximately 2 minutes.
5. Once the SORBET function has ended, turn the outer bowl and release it from the ninja CREAMi machine. 6. Your sorbet is ready to eat! Enjoy!

Squash Gelato

Prep time: 5 minutes | Cook time: 5 minutes | Serves 4

- 1¾ cups milk
- ½ cup cooked butternut squash
- ¼ cup granulated sugar
- ½ teaspoon ground cinnamon
- ¼ teaspoon ground allspice
- Pinch of salt

1. In a small saucepan, add all ingredients and beat until well combined.
2. Place the saucepan over medium heat and cook for about 5 minutes, stirring continuously.
3. Remove from the heat and transfer the mixture into an empty Ninja CREAMi pint container.
4. Place the container into an ice bath to cool. 5. After cooling, cover the container with the storage lid and freeze for 24 hours.
5. After 24 hours, remove the lid from container and arrange into the outer bowl of Ninja CREAMi.
6. Install the "Creamerizer Paddle" onto the lid of outer bowl.
7. Then rotate the lid clockwise to lock.
8. Press "Power" button to turn on the unit.
9. Then press "GELATO" button.
10. When the program is completed, turn the outer bowl and release it from the machine. 12. Transfer the gelato into serving bowls and serve immediately.

Blueberry & Crackers Gelato
Prep time: 10 minutes | Cook time: 3 minutes | Serves 4

- 4 large egg yolks
- 3 tablespoons granulated sugar
- 3 tablespoons wild blueberry preserves
- 1 teaspoon vanilla extract
- 1 cup whole milk
- ⅓ cup heavy cream
- ¼ cup cream cheese, softened
- 3-6 drops purple food coloring
- 2 large graham crackers, broken in 1-inch pieces

1. In a small saucepan, add the egg yolks, sugar, blueberry preserves and vanilla extract and beat until well combined.
2. Add the milk, heavy cream, cream cheese and food coloring and beat until well combined.
3. Place the saucepan over medium heat and cook for about 2-3 minutes, stirring continuously.
4. Remove from the heat and through a fine-mesh strainer, strain the mixture into an empty Ninja CREAMi pint container.
5. Place the container into an ice bath to cool.
6. After cooling, cover the container with the storage lid and freeze for 24 hours.
7. After 24 hours, remove the lid from container and arrange into the outer bowl of Ninja CREAMi.
8. Install the "Creamerizer Paddle" onto the lid of outer bowl.
9. Then rotate the lid clockwise to lock.
10. Press "Power" button to turn on the unit.
11. Then press "GELATO" button.
12. When the program is completed, with a spoon, create a 1½-inch wide hole in the center that reaches the bottom of the pint container.
13. Add the graham crackers into the hole and press "MIX-IN" button.
14. When the program is completed, turn the outer bowl and release it from the machine.
15. Transfer the gelato into serving bowls and serve immediately.

Easy Coconut Sorbet
Prep time: 5 minutes | Cook time:15 Minutes | Serves 6

- 1 cup coconut water
- ¾ cup sugar
- 2 cans coconut milk

1. Place coconut water and sugar in a saucepan. Bring to a boil until the sugar dissolves.
2. Remove from the heat and place in the fridge to chill for at least 3 hours.
3. Turn on the Cuisinart and pour in the water-sugar mixture and coconut milk.
4. Churn for 10 minutes.
5. Transfer in an airtight container and freeze overnight.

Blueberry & Pomegranate Sorbet
Prep time: 5 minutes | Cook time: 5 minutes | Serves 4

- 1 can blueberries in light syrup
- ½ cup pomegranate juice

1. In an empty Ninja CREAMi pint container, place the blueberries and top with syrup.
2. Add in the pomegranate juice and stir to combine.
3. Cover the container with the storage lid and freeze for 24 hours.
4. After 24 hours, remove the lid from container and arrange into the outer bowl of Ninja CREAMi.
5. Install the "Creamerizer Paddle" onto the lid of outer bowl.
6. Then rotate the lid clockwise to lock
7. Press "Power" button to turn on the unit.
8. Then press "SORBET" button.
9. When the program is completed, turn the outer bowl and release it from the machine. 10. Transfer the sorbet into serving bowls and serve immediately.

Strawberry & Beet Sorbet

Prep time: 5 minutes | Cook time: 5 minutes | Serves 4

- 2⅔ cups strawberries, hulled and quartered
- ⅓ cup cooked beets, quartered
- ⅓ cup granulated sugar
- ⅓ cup orange juice

1. In a high-speed blender, add mangoes and beets and pulse until smooth.
2. Through a fine-mesh strainer, strain the mango puree into a large bowl.
3. Add the sugar and orange juice and and stir to combine.
4. Transfer the mixture into an empty Ninja CREAMi pint container.
5. Cover the container with the storage lid and freeze for 24 hours.
6. After 24 hours, remove the lid from container and arrange into the outer bowl of Ninja CREAMi.
7. Install the "Creamerizer Paddle" onto the lid of outer bowl.
8. Then rotate the lid clockwise to lock.
9. Press "Power" button to turn on the unit.
10. Then press "SORBET" button.
11. When the program is completed, turn the outer bowl and release it from the machine. 12. Transfer the sorbet into serving bowls and serve immediately.

Strawberries & Champagne Sorbet

Prep time: 5 minutes | Cook time: 15 minutes | Serves 3

- 1 packet strawberry-flavored gelatin (such as Jell-O)
- ¾ cup boiling water
- ½ cup light corn syrup
- 3 fluid ounces champagne
- 1 egg whites, slightly beaten

1. Dissolve the gelatin in boiling water in a bowl. Beat in the corn syrup, champagne, and egg whites.
2. Put the mixture into the ninja CREAMi Pint container and freeze on a level surface in a cold freezer for a full 24 hours.
3. After 24 hours, remove the Pint from the freezer. Remove the lid.
4. Place the Ninja CREAMi Pint into the outer bowl. Place the outer bowl with the Pint in it into the ninja CREAMi machine and turn until the outer bowl locks into place. Push the SORBET button. During the SORBET function, the sorbet will mix together and become very creamy. This should take approximately 2 minutes.
5. Once the SORBET function has ended, turn the outer bowl and release it from the ninja CREAMi machine. 6. Your sorbet is ready to eat! Enjoy!

Strawberry Sorbet

Prep time: 5 minutes | Cook time: 5 minutes | Serves 4

- 6 ounces daiquiri mix
- 2 ounces rum
- ½ cup frozen strawberries
- ½ cup simple syrup

1. In an empty Ninja CREAMi pint container, add all the ingredients and mix well.
2. Cover the container with storage lid and freeze for 24 hours.
3. After 24 hours, remove the lid from container and arrange into the Outer Bowl of Ninja CREAMi. 4. Install the Creamerizer Paddle onto the lid of Outer Bowl.
4. Then rotate the lid clockwise to lock.
5. Press Power button to turn on the unit.
6. Then press Sorbet button.
7. When the program is completed, turn the Outer Bowl and release it from the machine. 9. Transfer the sorbet into serving bowls and serve immediately.

Pomegranate Sorbet Smile

Prep time: 5 minutes | Cook time: 45 minutes | Serves 4

- 1 pomegranate
- ½ cup white sugar
- 1½ tablespoons freshly squeezed lemon juice
- 1½ egg whites
- 1 cup heavy whipping cream

1. With a knife, score the pomegranate rinds lengthwise and crosswise. With the knife, carefully break open the fruit. Using the scored lines as a guide, cut the flesh into quarters with your hands. To release the seeds, hold each quarter over a big basin and beat it forcefully with a wooden spoon.
2. To release some liquid, crush the seeds in the basin with a potato masher. Continue mashing to release additional liquid after adding the sugar and lemon juice.
3. In a glass, metal, or ceramic bowl, whisk the egg whites until firm peaks form. Mash in the pomegranate mixture.
4. In a cold glass or metal bowl, beat the cream until thick. To get the correct consistency, mash it into the pomegranate mixture, popping the seeds as needed.
5. Put the mixture into the ninja CREAMi Pint container and freeze on a level surface in a cold freezer for a full 24 hours.
6. After 24 hours, remove the Pint from the freezer. Remove the lid.
7. Place the Ninja CREAMi Pint into the outer bowl. Place the outer bowl with the Pint in it into the ninja CREAMi machine and turn until the outer bowl locks into place. Push the SORBET button. During the SORBET function, the sorbet will mix together and become very creamy. This should take approximately 2 minutes.
8. Once the SORBET function has ended, turn the outer bowl and release it from the ninja CREAMi machine.
9. Your sorbet is ready to eat! Enjoy!

Chocolate Hazelnut Gelato

Prep time: 5 minutes | Cook time: 3 minutes | Serves 4

- 3 large egg yolks
- ⅓ cup hazelnut spread
- ¼ cup granulated sugar
- 2 teaspoons cocoa powder
- 1 tablespoon light corn syrup
- 1 cup whole milk
- ½ cup heavy cream
- 1 teaspoon vanilla extract

1. In a small saucepan, add the egg yolks, hazelnut spread, sugar, cocoa powder and corn syrup and beat until well combined.
2. Add the milk, heavy cream and vanilla extract and beat until well combined.
3. Place the saucepan over medium heat and cook for about 2-3 minutes, stirring continuously.
4. Remove from the heat and through a fine-mesh strainer, strain the mixture into an empty Ninja CREAMi pint container.
5. Place the container into an ice bath to cool.
6. After cooling, cover the container with the storage lid and freeze for 24 hours.
7. After 24 hours, remove the lid from container and arrange into the outer bowl of Ninja CREAMi.
8. Install the "Creamerizer Paddle" onto the lid of outer bowl.
9. Then rotate the lid clockwise to lock.
10. Press "Power" button to turn on the unit.
11. Then press "GELATO" button.
12. When the program is completed, turn the outer bowl and release it from the machine. 13. Transfer the gelato into serving bowls and serve immediately.

Sweet Potato Gelato

Prep time: 5 minutes | Cook time: 3 minutes | Serves 4

- ½ cup canned sweet potato puree
- 4 large egg yolks
- ¼ cup sugar
- ½ teaspoon ground cinnamon
- ⅛ teaspoon ground nutmeg
- 1 cup heavy cream
- 1 teaspoon vanilla extract

1. In a small saucepan, add the sweet potato puree, egg yolks, sugar, ½ teaspoon of cinnamon and nutmeg and beat until well combined.
2. Add the heavy cream and vanilla extract and beat until well combined.
3. Place the saucepan over medium heat and cook for about 2-3 minutes, stirring continuously.
4. Remove from the heat and through a fine-mesh strainer, strain the mixture into an empty Ninja CREAMi pint container.
5. Place the container into an ice bath to cool.
6. After cooling, cover the container with the storage lid and freeze for 24 hours.
7. After 24 hours, remove the lid from container and arrange into the outer bowl of Ninja CREAMi.
8. Install the "Creamerizer Paddle" onto the lid of outer bowl.
9. Then rotate the lid clockwise to lock.
10. Press "Power" button to turn on the unit.
11. Then press "GELATO" button.
12. When the program is completed, turn the outer bowl and release it from the machine. 13. Transfer the gelato into serving bowls and serve immediately.

Red Velvet Gelato

Prep time: 5 minutes | Cook time: 3 minutes | Serves 4

- 4 large egg yolks
- ¼ cup granulated sugar
- 2 tablespoons unsweetened cocoa powder
- 1 cup whole milk
- ⅓ cup heavy (whipping) cream
- ¼ cup cream cheese, at room temperature
- 1 teaspoon vanilla extract
- 1 teaspoon red food coloring

1. Fill a large bowl with ice water and set it aside.
2. In a small saucepan, whisk together the egg yolks, sugar, and cocoa powder until everything is fully combined and the sugar is dissolved. Do not do this over heat.
3. Whisk in the milk, heavy cream, cream cheese, vanilla, and food coloring.
4. Place the pan over medium heat. Cook, stirring constantly with a rubber spatula, until the temperature reaches 165°F to 175°F on an instant-read thermometer.
5. Remove the pan from the heat and pour the base through a fine-mesh strainer into a clean CREAMi Pint. Carefully place the container in the prepared ice water bath, making sure the water doesn't spill into the base.
6. Once the base has cooled, place the storage lid on the pint and freeze for 24 hours.
7. Remove the pint from the freezer and take off the lid. Place the pint in the outer bowl of your Ninja CREAMi, install the Creamerizer Paddle in the outer bowl lid, and lock the lid assembly onto the outer bowl. Place the bowl assembly on the motor base, and twist the handle to the right to raise the platform and lock it in place. Select the Gelato function.
8. Once the machine has finished processing, remove the gelato from the pint. Serve immediately.

Chapter 5
Milkshake Recipes

Chocolate Cherry Cocoa Banana Vegan Milkshake

Prep time: 5 minutes | Cook time:10 Minutes | Serves 9

- 3/4 cup water
- 1 1/4 cups full fat coconut milk or coconut cream (as thick as possible)
- 2/3 cup organic cane sugar
- 2/3 cup unsweetened cocoa powder
- 1/4 tsp sea salt
- 6 oz. vegan dark chocolate, finely chopped
- 1/2 tsp pure vanilla extract
- ¼ cup sliced frozen bananas
- ¼ cup cherries (cut up fine)
- 1 tbsp. cinnamon

1. Put the first 5 ingredients in a large saucepan, and heat it on medium-high heat. Mix the ingredients together using a whisk. Allow the mixture to come to a low boil. Continue to whisk often, and remain cooking on a low boil for 1 minute.
2. Take the pan off the heat, and mix in the chocolate and vanilla extract using the whisk. Continue to mix until the chocolate is melted. Add cherries and cinnamon.
3. Place the mixture in a blender with the bananas, and blend on high speed for about 30 seconds, then allow the mixture to cool
4. Pour the ingredients into your ice cream maker, and let it churn for 10-15 minutes, until desired consistency is reached and serve immediately.

Mango Strawberry Mint Daiquiri Milkshake

Prep time: 5 minutes | Cook time:25 Minutes | Serves 6

- 2 cups heavy cream
- 1 cup milk
- 3/4 cup sugar
- 8 ounces strawberries
- ¼ cup mint
- ¼ cup mango
- 4 tablespoons rum

1. Puree the strawberries, mango and mint in a food processor or blender.
2. Place the milk and cream in a bowl, and mix them together until well combined. Use a whisk to mix in the sugar. Continue to whisk for about 4 minutes until the sugar dissolves. Then mix in the rum, and strawberry puree.
3. Pour the ingredients into your ice cream maker, and let it churn for 10-15 minutes, until desired consistency is reached. About 5 minutes before the ice cream is done churning add the peanut butter cup to your ice cream maker.
4. Serve immediately.

Chocolate-peanut Butter Milkshake

Prep time: 5 minutes | Cook time: 3 minutes | Serves 2

- 1½ cups chocolate ice cream
- ½ cup whole milk
- ¼ cup mini peanut butter cups

1. Combine the chocolate ice cream and milk in a clean CREAMi Pint.
2. Use a spoon to create a 1½-inch-wide hole that goes all the way to the bottom of the pint. Pour the mini peanut butter cups into the hole.
3. Place the pint in the outer bowl of your Ninja CREAMi, install the Creamerizer Paddle in the outer bowl lid, and lock the lid assembly onto the outer bowl. Place the bowl assembly on the motor base, and twist the handle to the right to raise the platform and lock it in place. Select the Milkshake function.
4. Once the machine has finished processing, remove the milkshake from the pint. Serve immediately.

Amaretto Cookies Milkshake

Prep time: 5 minutes | Cook time: 3 minutes | Serves 2

- 1 cup whole milk
- ½ cup amaretto-flavored coffee creamer
- ¼ cup amaretto liqueur
- 1 tablespoon agave nectar
- ¼ cup chocolate chip cookies, chopped

1. In an empty Ninja CREAMi pint container, place all ingredients except for cookies and stir to combine.
2. Cover the container with the storage lid and freeze for 24 hours.
3. After 24 hours, remove the lid from container and arrange into the outer bowl of Ninja CREAMi.
4. Install the "Creamerizer Paddle" onto the lid of outer bowl.
5. Then rotate the lid clockwise to lock.
6. Press "Power" button to turn on the unit.
7. Then press "MILKSHAKE" button.
8. When the program is completed, with a spoon, create a 1½-inch wide hole in the center that reaches the bottom of the pint container.
9. Add the chopped cookies into the hole and press "MIX-IN" button.
10. When the program is completed, turn the outer bowl and release it from the machine. 11. Transfer the shake into serving glasses and serve immediately.

Chocolate Liqueur Milkshake

Prep time: 5 minutes | Cook time: 3 minutes | Serves 2

- 2 cups vanilla ice cream
- ⅓ cup chocolate liqueur
- ⅓ cup whole milk

1. In an empty Ninja CREAMi pint container, place ice cream, followed by chocolate liqueur and milk.
2. Arrange the container into the outer bowl of Ninja CREAMi.
3. Install the "Creamerizer Paddle" onto the lid of outer bowl.
4. Then rotate the lid clockwise to lock.
5. Press "Power" button to turn on the unit.
6. Then press "MILKSHAKE" button.
7. When the program is completed, turn the outer bowl and release it from the machine. 8. Transfer the shake into serving glasses and serve immediately.

Hazelnut Milkshake

Prep time: 5 minutes | Cook time: 5 minute | Serves 2

- 1½ cups hazelnut ice cream
- ½ cup whole milk
- ¼ cup chocolate spread

1. Move all the ingredients into a CREAMi pint container and merge well.
2. Fasten the lid of the pint and freeze for 24 hours.
3. After 24 hours, open the pint, fix it into the outer bowl of Ninja CREAMi along with the 'Creamerizer paddle'.
4. Fasten the lid, turn on the 'Power Button', and select the 'MILKSHAKE' function.
5. Ladle out the shake into serving glasses and serve chilled.

Marshmallow Oat Milkshake

Prep time: 10 minutes | Cook time: 5 minute | Serves 2

- 1½ cups vanilla ice cream
- ½ cup oat milk
- ½ cup marshmallow cereal

1. Move the ice cream, oat milk, and marshmallow cereal into a CREAMi pint container. 2. Fasten the lid of the pint and freeze for 24 hours.
2. After 24 hours, open the pint, fix it into the outer bowl of Ninja CREAMi along with the 'Creamerizer paddle'.
3. Fasten the lid, turn on the 'Power Button', and select the 'MILKSHAKE' function.
4. Ladle out the shake into serving glasses and serve chilled.

Pumpkin Pie Milkshake

Prep time: 5 minutes | Cook time: 5 minutes| Serves 2

- 3/4 cup (185 g) pumpkin puree
- 2 scoops (120 g) vanilla ice cream
- 1 tablespoon (7 g) chopped walnuts
- 1/4 teaspoon (0.5 g) pumpkin pie spice
- 1 cup (250 ml) almond milk, unsweetened
- Pumpkin seeds, for garnish (optional)

1. Combine the pumpkin puree, vanilla ice cream, walnuts, pumpkin pie spice, and almond milk in a blender. Process until it becomes smooth.
2. Pour mixture into 2 chilled glasses. Garnish with some pumpkin seeds, if desired.
3. Serve and enjoy!

Cacao Mint Milkshake

Prep time: 5 minutes | Cook time: 3 minutes | Serves 2

- 1½ cups vanilla ice cream
- ½ cup canned full-fat coconut milk
- 1 teaspoon matcha powder
- ¼ cup cacao nibs
- 1 teaspoon peppermint extract

1. In an empty Ninja CREAMi pint container, place ice cream followed by coconut milk, matcha powder, cacao nibs and peppermint extract.
2. Arrange the container into the Outer Bowl of Ninja CREAMi.
3. Install the Creamerizer Paddle onto the lid of Outer Bowl.
4. Then rotate the lid clockwise to lock.
5. Press Power button to turn on the unit.
6. Then press Milkshake button.
7. When the program is completed, turn the Outer Bowl and release it from the machine. 8. Transfer the shake into serving glasses and serve immediately.

Pumpkin Latte Milkshake

Prep time: 10 minutes | Cook time: 5 minute | Serves 4

- 2 cups whole milk
- 2 tablespoons sugar, granulated
- 1 cup coffee, brewed
- 4 cups vanilla ice cream
- ½ cup pumpkin puree, canned
- 1 teaspoon pumpkin pie spice
- 2 teaspoons vanilla extract
- 1 cup ice cubes

1. In a saucepan, lightly boil the milk and then ladle out in a mixing bowl.
2. Merge in the pumpkin, sugar, pumpkin pie spice, coffee, and vanilla essence.
3. Whisk well and refrigerate for an hour.
4. Move the mixture into a CREAMi pint container along with vanilla ice cream.
5. Fasten the lid of the pint and freeze for 24 hours.
6. After 24 hours, open the pint, fix it into the outer bowl of Ninja CREAMi along with the 'Creamerizer paddle'.
7. Fasten the lid, turn on the 'Power Button', and select the 'MILKSHAKE' function.
8. Ladle out the shake into serving glasses and serve chilled.

Cashew Chocolate Milkshake

Prep time: 10 minutes | Cook time: 5 minute | Serves 2

- ½ cup cashew milk
- 1½ cups chocolate ice cream
- ½ cup ripe banana, cut into pieces
- 1 tablespoon instant coffee powder

1. Move all the ingredients into a CREAMi pint container except the chocolate chip cookies.
2. Fasten the lid of the pint and freeze for 24 hours.
3. After 24 hours, open the pint, fix it into the outer bowl of Ninja CREAMi along with the 'Creamerizer paddle'.
4. Fasten the lid, turn on the 'Power Button', and select the 'MILKSHAKE' function.
5. Ladle out the shake into serving glasses and serve chilled.

Creamy Strawberry Banana Milkshake

Prep time: 5 minutes | Cook time: 5 minutes| Serves 2

- 1 cup (220 g) frozen strawberries, hulled
- 1 large (180 g) frozen banana, cut into small pieces
- 2 scoops (120 g) vanilla ice cream
- 1 cup (250 ml) skim milk
- Fresh mint sprigs

1. Combine the frozen strawberries, banana, vanilla ice cream, and milk in a blender. Process until it becomes smooth.
2. Pour mixture into 2 chilled glasses. Garnish with some strawberries and mint sprigs.
3. Enjoy.

Pink Raspberry Almond Milkshake

Prep time: 5 minutes | Cook time: 5 minutes| Serves 2

- 1 cup (250 g) frozen raspberries, plus more for garnish
- 1 cup (250 g) almond milk
- 1 scoop (60 g) vanilla ice cream
- 1 tablespoon (15 ml) peppermint syrup
- Fresh mint sprigs

1. Combine the raspberries, almond milk, vanilla ice cream, and peppermint syrup in a blender. Process until smooth and creamy.
2. Transfer mixture into 2 chilled glasses. Garnish with raspberries and mint sprigs.
3. Enjoy!

Chocolate Hazelnut Milkshake

Prep time: 5 minutes | Cook time: 5 minutes| Serves 2

- 2 scoops (120 g) chocolate flavored ice cream
- 1 cup (250 ml) skim milk
- 2 tablespoons (30 ml) hazelnut syrup
- 6 ice cubes
- Whipped cream
- Chocolate shavings

1. Combine the ice cream, milk, hazelnut syrup, and ice cubes in a blender. Process until it becomes smooth.
2. Pour mixture into 2 chilled glasses. Add some whipped cream and chocolate shavings on top.
3. Enjoy!

Vegan Chocolate Banana Milkshake

Prep time: 5 minutes | Cook time: 5 minute | Serves 2

- ½ cup cashew milk
- 1½ cups vegan chocolate ice cream
- ½ cup fresh banana, ripe
- 1 tablespoon coffee powder, instant

1. Move the ice cream into a CREAMi pint container.
2. Use a spoon to make a hole that is 1½ inches wide in the pint's bottom.
3. Add the remaining ingredients to the hole.
4. Fasten the lid of the pint and freeze for 24 hours.
5. After 24 hours, open the pint, fix it into the outer bowl of Ninja CREAMi along with the 'Creamerizer paddle'.
6. Fasten the lid, turn on the 'Power Button', and select the 'MILKSHAKE' function.
7. Ladle out the shake into serving glasses and serve chilled.

Chocolate Ice Cream Milkshake

Prep time: 5 minutes | Cook time: 3 minutes | Serves 1

- 1½ cups chocolate ice cream
- ½ cup whole milk

1. In an empty Ninja CREAMi pint container, place ice cream, followed by milk.
2. Arrange the container into the Outer Bowl of Ninja CREAMi.
3. Install the Creamerizer Paddle onto the lid of Outer Bowl.
4. Then rotate the lid clockwise to lock. 5. Press Power button to turn on the unit. 6. Then press Milkshake button. 7. When the program is completed, turn the Outer Bowl and release it from the machine. 8. Transfer the shake into a serving glass and serve immediately.

Banana Apricot and Oat Milkshake

Prep time: 5 minutes | Cook time: 5 minutes | Serves 2

- 1 large (180 g) frozen banana, cut into small pieces
- 2 scoops (120 g) vanilla ice cream
- 1 cup (250 ml) whole milk
- 1/2 cup (85 g) apricots, diced
- 2 tablespoons (15 g) rolled oats, plus more for garnish
- Fresh mint sprigs

1. Combine the banana, ice cream, milk, apricots, oats, and ice cubes in a high-speed blender. Process until smooth and creamy.
2. Pour into 2 chilled glasses. Garnish with some oats and mint sprigs.
3. Serve and enjoy.

Mixed Berries Milkshake

Prep time: 5 minutes | Cook time: 3 minutes | Serves 2

- 1½ cups vanilla ice cream
- ½ cup milk
- ½ cup fresh mixed berries

1. In an empty Ninja CREAMi pint container, place ice cream followed by milk and berries.
2. Arrange the container into the outer bowl of Ninja CREAMi.
3. Install the Creamerizer Paddle onto the lid of Outer Bowl.
4. Then rotate the lid clockwise to lock. 5. Press Power button to turn on the unit. 6. Then press Milkshake button. 7. When the program is completed, turn the Outer Bowl and release it from the machine. 8. Transfer the shake into serving glasses and serve immediately.

Peanut Butter And Jelly Milkshake

Prep time: 5 minutes | Cook time: 5 minutes | Serves 2

- 3 tablespoons peanut butter
- 3 tablespoons grape jelly
- 1 cup milk
- 5 ice cubes
- ½ teaspoon vanilla extract

1. Add the milk, peanut butter, ice cubes, vanilla extract, and grape jelly into an empty CREAMi Pint.
2. Place the Pint in the outer bowl, install the Creamerizer Paddle onto the outer bowl lid and lock the lid assembly on the outer bowl. Place the bowl assembly on the motor base and crank the lever to elevate and secure the platform in place.
3. Choose the MILKSHAKE option.
4. Remove the milkshake from the Pint after the processing is finished.

Orange Milkshake

Prep time: 5 minutes | Cook time: 5 minutes | Serves 1

- 1 cup orange juice
- 2 scoops vanilla ice cream
- ½ cup milk
- 2 teaspoons white sugar

1. Place orange juice, ice cream, milk, and sugar in an empty CREAMi Pint.
2. Place Pint in outer bowl, install Creamerizer Paddle onto outer bowl lid and lock the lid assembly on the outer bowl. Place the bowl assembly on the motor base and crank the lever to elevate and secure the platform in place.
3. Select MILKSHAKE.
4. Remove the milkshake from the Pint after the processing is finished.

Chocolate Yogurt Milkshake

Prep time: 5 minutes | Cook time: 3 minutes | Serves 2

- 1 cup frozen chocolate yogurt
- 1 scoop chocolate whey protein powder
- 1 cup whole milk

1. In an empty Ninja CREAMi pint container, place yogurt followed by protein powder and milk.
2. Arrange the container into the Outer Bowl of Ninja CREAMi.
3. Install the Creamerizer Paddle onto the lid of Outer Bowl.
4. Then rotate the lid clockwise to lock. 5. Press Power button to turn on the unit. 6. Then press Milkshake button. 7. When the program is completed, turn the Outer Bowl and release it from the machine. 8. Transfer the shake into serving glasses and serve immediately.

Lemon Cookie Milkshake

Prep time: 8 minutes | Cook time: 3 minutes | Serves 2

- 1½ cups vanilla ice cream
- 3 lemon cream sandwich cookies
- ¼ cup milk

1. In an empty Ninja CREAMi pint container, place ice cream followed by cookies and milk.
2. Arrange the container into the Outer Bowl of Ninja CREAMi.
3. Install the Creamerizer Paddle onto the lid of Outer Bowl.
4. Then rotate the lid clockwise to lock. 5. Press Power button to turn on the unit. 6. Then press Milkshake button. 7. When the program is completed, turn the Outer Bowl and release it from the machine. 8. Transfer the shake into serving glasses and serve immediately.

Chapter 6
Ice Cream Mix-ins

Snack Mix Ice Cream

Prep time: 5 minutes | Cook time: 10 seconds | Serves 4

- 1 tablespoon cream cheese, softened
- ⅓ cup granulated sugar
- ½ teaspoon vanilla extract
- 1 cup whole milk
- ¾ cup heavy cream
- 2 tablespoons sugar cone pieces
- 1 tablespoon mini pretzels
- 1 tablespoon potato chips, crushed

1. In a large microwave-safe bowl, add the cream cheese and microwave on High for about ten seconds.
2. Remove from the microwave and stir until smooth.
3. Add the sugar and vanilla extract and with a wire whisk, beat until the mixture looks like frosting.
4. Slowly add the milk and heavy cream and beat until well combined.
5. Transfer the mixture into an empty Ninja CREAMi pint container.
6. Cover the container with storage lid and freeze for 24 hours.
7. After 24 hours, remove the lid from container and arrange into the Outer Bowl of Ninja CREAMi.
8. Install the Creamerizer Paddle onto the lid of Outer Bowl.
9. Then rotate the lid clockwise to lock.
10. Press Power button to turn on the unit.
11. Then press Ice Cream button.
12. When the program is completed, with a spoon, create a 1½-inch wide hole in the center that reaches the bottom of the pint container.
13. Add the cone pieces, pretzels and potato chips into the hole and press Mix-In button. 14. When the program is completed, turn the Outer Bowl and release it from the machine.
14. Transfer the ice cream into serving bowls and serve immediately.

Sweet Lemon Ice Cream

Prep Time: 10 minutes |Cooking Time: 24 Hours 20 Minutes | Serves 5

- 1 cup heavy whipping cream
- ½ cup half and half cream
- ½ cup white sugar
- 1 tablespoon lemon zest, grated
- 2 egg yolks
- ¼ cup fresh lemon juice

1. On low heat, whisk together the heavy cream, half-and-half cream, sugar, and lemon zest in a saucepan until the sugar is dissolved (about 5 minutes).
2. In a mixing dish, whisk together the egg yolks.
3. Stir in a few tablespoons of the cream mixture at a time into the eggs. This will assist in bringing the eggs up to temperature without them becoming scrambled. Return the egg mixture to the bowl with the cream mixture. (5 to 10 minutes of stirring until the mixture is frothy.)
4. Pour the mixture into an empty ninja CREAMi Pint container, add lemon, and freeze for 24 hours.
5. After 24 hours, remove the Pint from the freezer. Remove the lid.
6. Place the Ninja CREAMi Pint into the outer bowl. Next, place the outer bowl with the Pint into the ninja CREAMi machine and turn until the outer bowl locks into place. Then, push the ICE CREAM button.
7. Once the ICE CREAM function has ended, turn the outer bowl and release it from the ninja CREAMi machine.

The Golden Rocky Road
Prep Time: 10 minutes |Cooking Time: 24 hours | Serves 2

- ½ cup whole milk
- ¼ cup frozen cauliflower florets, thawed
- ¼ cup dark brown sugar
- 1 tablespoon dark cocoa powder
- ½ teaspoon chocolate extract
- ¼ cup heavy cream
- 1 tablespoon sliced almonds
- 1 tablespoon mini chocolate chip
- 1 tablespoon mini marshmallow, mix in

1. In a blender pitcher, combine the milk, cauliflower, brown sugar, cocoa powder, and chocolate essence. Blend on high for about 60 seconds, or until the mixture is totally smooth.
2. Pour the base into an empty CREAMi Pint. Add heavy cream and stir until well combined. Place the storage lid on the Pint and freeze for 24 hours.
3. Remove the Pint from the freezer and remove the lid from the Pint. Place Pint in outer bowl, install Creamerizer Paddle onto outer bowl lid and lock the lid assembly on the outer bowl. Select ICE CREAM.
4. With a spoon, create a life-inch wide hole that reaches the bottom of the Pint. Add the sliced almonds, chocolate chips, and marshmallows to the hole and process using the MIX-IN program.
5. When processing is complete, remove the ice cream from the Pint and serve immediately.

Homely Peanut Butter Ice Cream
Prep Time: 10 minutes | Cook time: 25 minutes | Serves 2

- 1 and ¾ cup skim milk
- 3 tablespoons smooth peanut butter
- ¼ cup stevia-cane sugar blend
- 1 teaspoon vanilla extract

1. In a bowl, add all Ingredients and beat until smooth.
2. Set aside for about five minutes.
3. Transfer the mixture into an empty Ninja CREAMi pint container.
4. Cover the container with a storage lid and freeze for 24 hours.
5. After 24 hours, remove the lid from the container and arrange it into the outer bowl of Ninja CREAMi.
6. Install the Creamerizer Paddle onto the lid of the Outer Bowl.
7. Then rotate the lid clockwise to lock.
8. Press the Power button to turn on the unit.
9. Then press the Ice Cream button.
10. When the program is completed, turn the Outer Bowl and release it from the machine.
11. Transfer the ice cream into serving bowls and serve.

Hearty Strawberry Ice Cream

Prep Time: 10 minutes | Cook time: 24 Hours and 5 Minutes | Serves 2

- 1 tablespoon cream cheese
- ¼ cup sugar
- 1 teaspoon vanilla bean paste
- ¾ cup heavy whipping cream
- 1 cup milk
- 6 strawberries

1. In a mixing dish, combine the cream cheese, sugar, and vanilla bean paste. Using a whisk, blend all ingredients until they are thoroughly mixed and the sugar begins to dissolve.
2. Combine the heavy whipping cream and milk in a mixing bowl. Whisk until all of the ingredients are thoroughly blended.
3. Pour the mixture into an empty ninja CREAMi Pint container. Freeze for 24 hours after adding the strawberries to the Pint, ensuring not to go over the maximum fill line.
4. Take the Pint out of the freezer after 24 hours. Take off the lid.
5. Place the Ninja CREAMi Pint into the outer bowl. Next, place the outer bowl with the Pint into the ninja CREAMi machine and turn until the outer bowl locks into place. Then, push the ICE CREAM button. During the ICE CREAM function, the ice cream will mix and become very creamy.
6. Once the ICE CREAM function has ended, turn the outer bowl and release it from the ninja CREAMi machine.
7. Your ice cream is ready to eat! Enjoy!

Creamy Cookie Ice Cream

Prep time: 40 minutes | Cook time: 5 minutes | Serves 2

- 1 cup frosted cookies, crushed, divided
- ½ cup whole milk
- ½ tablespoon cream cheese, softened
- 1 teaspoon vanilla extract
- 4 tablespoons sugar, granulated
- ¼ cup heavy cream

1. In a bowl, merge together the milk and 1 cup of crushed cookies. Let it rest for 30 minutes.
2. In a large microwave-safe bowl, microwave the cream cheese for 12 seconds.
3. Merge together the granulated sugar and vanilla extract.
4. Sift the cookie mixture over the cream cheese mixture.
5. Fold in the heavy cream and whisk well.
6. Move the mixture into an empty Ninja CREAMI pint.
7. Fasten the lid of the pint and freeze for 24 hours.
8. After 24 hours, open the pint, fix it into the outer bowl of Ninja CREAMi along with the 'Creamerizer paddle'
9. Fasten the lid, turn on the 'Power Button', and select the 'ICE CREAM'' function.
10. Now, make a wide hole in the center that reaches the bottom of the pint.
11. Put the remaining crushed cookies in the hole and select the "MIX-IN" function.
12. Dish out the ice cream from the pint and serve chilled.

Pistachio Ice Cream

Prep time: 15 minutes | Cook time: 5 minutes| Serves 4

- ⅓ cup sugar, granulated
- 1 tablespoon cream cheese, softened
- 1 teaspoon almond extract
- ¾ cup heavy cream
- 1 cup whole milk
- ¼ cup pistachios, shells removed and chopped

1. In a large microwave-safe bowl, microwave the cream cheese for 12 seconds.
2. Add the sugar and almond extract and thoroughly whisk.
3. Slowly fold in the heavy cream and milk until completely smooth.
4. Move the mixture into an empty Ninja CREAMI pint.
5. Fasten the lid of the pint and freeze for 24 hours.
6. After 24 hours, open the pint, fix it into the outer bowl of Ninja CREAMi along with the 'Creamerizer paddle'
7. Fasten the lid, turn on the 'Power Button', and select the 'ICE CREAM'' function.
8. Now, make a wide hole in the center that reaches the bottom of the pint.
9. Put the pistachios in the hole and select the "MIX-IN" function.
10. Dish out the ice cream from the pint and serve chilled.

Chocolate Walnuts Ice Cream

Prep time: 10 minutes | Cook time: 5 minutes| Serves 4

- ⅓ cup sugar
- 1 tablespoon cream cheese, softened
- 1 teaspoon banana extract
- 1 cup whole milk
- 2 tablespoons walnuts, for mix-in
- ¾ cup heavy cream
- 2 tablespoons chocolate chunks, for mix-in

1. In a large microwave-safe bowl, microwave the cream cheese for 12 seconds.
2. Add the sugar and banana extract and thoroughly whisk.
3. Slowly fold in the heavy cream and milk until completely smooth.
4. Move the mixture into an empty Ninja CREAMI pint.
5. Fasten the lid of the pint and freeze for 24 hours.
6. After 24 hours, open the pint, fix it into the outer bowl of Ninja CREAMi along with the 'Creamerizer paddle'
7. Fasten the lid, turn on the 'Power Button', and select the 'ICE CREAM'' function.
8. Now, make a wide hole in the center that reaches the bottom of the pint.
9. Put the chocolate chunks and walnuts in the hole and select the "MIX-IN" function.
10. Dish out the ice cream from the pint and serve chilled.

Triple-chocolate Ice Cream

Prep time: 5 minutes | Cook time: 3 minutes | Serves 4

- 4 large egg yolks
- ⅓ cup granulated sugar
- 1 tablespoon unsweetened cocoa powder
- 1 tablespoon hot fudge sauce
- ¾ cup heavy (whipping) cream
- ½ cup whole milk
- 1 teaspoon vanilla extract
- ¼ cup white chocolate chips

1. Fill a large bowl with ice water and set it aside.
2. In a small saucepan, whisk together the egg yolks, sugar, and cocoa powder until the mixture is fully combined and the sugar is dissolved. Do not do this over heat.
3. Whisk in the hot fudge, heavy cream, milk, and vanilla.
4. Place the pan over medium heat. Cook, stirring constantly with a rubber spatula, until the temperature reaches 165°F to 175°F on an instant-read thermometer.
5. Remove the pan from the heat and pour the base through a fine-mesh strainer into a clean CREAMi Pint. Carefully place the container in the prepared ice water bath, making sure the water doesn't spill into the base.
6. Once the base has cooled, place the storage lid on the pint and freeze for 24 hours.
7. Remove the pint from the freezer and take off the lid. Place the pint in the outer bowl of your Ninja CREAMi, install the Creamerizer Paddle in the outer bowl lid, and lock the lid assembly onto the outer bowl. Place the bowl assembly on the motor base, and twist the handle to the right to raise the platform and lock it in place. Select the Ice Cream function.
8. Once the machine has finished processing, remove the lid from the pint container. With a spoon, create a 1½-inch-wide hole that reaches the bottom of the pint. During this process, it is okay if your treat reaches above the Max Fill line. Add the white chocolate chips to the hole in the pint, replace the lid, and select the Mix-In function.
9. Once the machine has finished processing, remove the ice cream from the pint. Serve immediately with desired toppings.

Tooti Fruity Extract Ice Cream

Prep Time: 10 minutes | Cook time: 25 minutes | Serves 2

- 1 cup whole milk
- ¾ cup heavy cream
- 2 tablespoons monk fruit sweetener
- 2 tablespoons agave nectar
- ½ teaspoon raspberry extract
- ½ teaspoon vanilla extract
- ¼ teaspoon lemon extract
- 5-6 drops of blue food color

1. In a bowl, add all Ingredients and eat until well combined.
2. Transfer the mixture into an empty Ninja CREAMi pint container.
3. Cover the container with a storage lid and freeze for 24 hours.
4. After 24 hours, remove the lid from the container and arrange it into the Outer Bowl of Ninja CREAMi.
5. Install the Creamerizer Paddle onto the lid of the outer bowl.
6. Then rotate the lid clockwise to lock.
7. Press the Power button to turn on the unit.
8. Then press the Ice Cream button.
9. When the program is completed, turn the Outer Bowl and release it from the machine.
10. Transfer the ice cream into serving bowls and serve immediately.

Butter Cookies Ice Cream

Prep time: 10 minutes | Cook time: 5 minutes | Serves 3

- ¼ teaspoon vanilla extract
- 1 tablespoon butter, unsalted
- ½ cup light brown sugar
- 2 cups heavy whipping cream
- ¼ cup crushed cookies

1. In a saucepan over medium heat, merge together all the ingredients except for crushed cookies.
2. Cook for about 5 minutes and then eliminate from the heat.
3. Refrigerate for at least 4 hours.
4. Move the mixture into an empty Ninja CREAMI pint.
5. Fasten the lid of the pint and freeze for 24 hours.
6. After 24 hours, open the pint, fix it into the outer bowl of Ninja CREAMi along with the 'Creamerizer paddle'
7. Fasten the lid, turn on the 'Power Button', and select the 'ICE CREAM'' function.
8. Now, make a wide hole in the center that reaches the bottom of the pint.
9. Put the crushed cookies in the hole and select the "MIX-IN" function.
10. Dish out the ice cream from the pint and serve chilled.

Strawberry Oreo Ice Cream

Prep time: 5 minutes | Cook time: 5 minutes | Serves 4

- ⅓ cup sugar, granulated
- 1 tablespoon cream cheese, softened
- 1 teaspoon vanilla extract
- ¾ cup heavy cream, whipped
- 6 oreos, broken
- 6 strawberries, chopped
- 1 cup whole milk

1. In a large microwave-safe bowl, microwave the cream cheese for 12 seconds.
2. Add the sugar, vanilla extract and strawberries and thoroughly whisk.
3. Slowly fold in the heavy cream and milk until completely smooth.
4. Move the mixture into an empty Ninja CREAMI pint.
5. Fasten the lid of the pint and freeze for 24 hours.
6. After 24 hours, open the pint, fix it into the outer bowl of Ninja CREAMi along with the 'Creamerizer paddle'
7. Fasten the lid, turn on the 'Power Button', and select the 'ICE CREAM'' function.
8. Now, make a wide hole in the center that reaches the bottom of the pint.
9. Put the broken oreos in the hole and select the "MIX-IN" function.
10. Dish out the ice cream from the pint and serve chilled.

Coconut Mint Chip Ice Cream

Prep time: 5 minutes | Cook time: 3 minutes | Serves 4

- 1 can full-fat unsweetened coconut milk
- ½ cup organic sugar
- ½ teaspoon mint extract
- ¼ cup mini vegan chocolate chips

1. In a medium bowl, whisk together the coconut milk, sugar, and mint extract until everything is well combined and the sugar is dissolved.
2. Pour the base into a clean CREAMi Pint. Place the storage lid on the container and freeze for 24 hours.
3. Remove the pint from the freezer and take off the lid. Place the pint in the outer bowl of your Ninja CREAMi, install the Creamerizer Paddle in the outer bowl lid, and lock the lid assembly onto the outer bowl. Place the bowl assembly on the motor base, and twist the handle to the right to raise the platform and lock it in place. Select the Ice Cream function.
4. Once the machine has finished processing, remove the lid from the pint container. With a spoon, create a 1½-inch-wide hole that reaches the bottom of the pint. During this process, it is okay if your treat reaches above the Max Fill line. Add the mini chocolate chips to the hole in the pint, replace the lid, and select the Mix-In function.
5. Once the machine has finished processing, remove the ice cream from the pint. Serve immediately with desired toppings.

Pecan and Potato Chips Ice Cream

Prep time: 10 minutes | Cook time: 5 minutes | Serves 6

- ¾ cup heavy cream
- 1 cup whole milk
- ⅓ cup sugar, granulated
- 5 pecan shortbread cookies
- ½ cup pecans, toasted and coarsely chopped
- ½ cup potato chips, crushed

1. In a blender, blitz pecans with the remaining ingredients except for potato chips.
2. Move the mixture into an empty Ninja CREAMI pint.
3. Fasten the lid of the pint and freeze for 24 hours.
4. After 24 hours, open the pint, fix it into the outer bowl of Ninja CREAMi along with the 'Creamerizer paddle'
5. Fasten the lid, turn on the 'Power Button', and select the 'ICE CREAM" function.
6. Now, make a wide hole in the center that reaches the bottom of the pint.
7. Put the potato chips in the hole and select the "MIX-IN" function.
8. Dish out the ice cream from the pint and serve chilled.

Blueberry Ice cream

Prep time: 10 minutes | Cook time: 5 minutes| Serves 6

- 1 cup whole milk
- 6 pie crusts
- ¾ cup heavy cream
- 1 large egg, beaten
- ¾ cup frozen blueberries, thawed
- ⅓ cup sugar, granulated

1. In a blender, blitz half of the blueberries with the remaining ingredients in it.
2. Move the mixture into an empty Ninja CREAMI pint.
3. Fasten the lid of the pint and freeze for 24 hours.
4. After 24 hours, open the pint, fix it into the outer bowl of Ninja CREAMi along with the 'Creamerizer paddle'
5. Fasten the lid, turn on the 'Power Button', and select the 'ICE CREAM'' function.
6. Now, make a wide hole in the center that reaches the bottom of the pint.
7. Put the remaining blueberries in the hole and select the "MIX-IN" function.
8. Dish out the ice cream from the pint and serve chilled.

Chocolate-Spinach Ice Cream

Prep time: 15 minutes | Cook time: 5 minutes| Serves 4

- 1 cup whole milk
- ½ cup frozen spinach, thawed and squeezed dry
- ½ cup sugar, granulated
- 4 drops green food coloring
- ¼ cup chocolate chunks, chopped
- 1 teaspoon mint extract
- ⅓ cup heavy cream
- ¼ cup brownie, cut into 1-inch pieces

1. In a blender, blitz the spinach, milk, sugar, mint extract and food coloring in it.
2. Move the mixture into an empty Ninja CREAMI pint.
3. Add the heavy cream and stir thoroughly.
4. Fasten the lid of the pint and freeze for 24 hours.
5. After 24 hours, open the pint, fix it into the outer bowl of Ninja CREAMi along with the 'Creamerizer paddle'
6. Fasten the lid, turn on the 'Power Button', and select the 'ICE CREAM'' function.
7. Now, make a wide hole in the center that reaches the bottom of the pint.
8. Put the chocolate chunks and brownie pieces in the hole and select the "MIX-IN" function.
9. Dish out the ice cream from the pint and serve chilled.

Peas and Berries Ice Cream

Prep time: 5 minutes | Cook time: 5 minutes| Serves 4

- ½ cup frozen peas, thawed
- 3 tablespoons grape jam
- ¾ cup whole milk
- ¼ cup sugar, granulated
- 1 teaspoon vanilla extract
- ½ cup heavy cream
- ¼ cup frozen mixed berries, for mix-in
- 2 tablespoons peanut butter powder
- 7 drops purple gel food coloring
- ¼ cup roasted peanuts, chopped, for mix-in

1. In a blender, blitz the milk, peas, sugar, grape jam, peanut butter powder, food coloring and vanilla extract in it.
2. Move the mixture into an empty Ninja CREAMI pint.
3. Add the heavy cream and stir thoroughly.
4. Fasten the lid of the pint and freeze for 24 hours.
5. After 24 hours, open the pint, fix it into the outer bowl of Ninja CREAMi along with the 'Creamerizer paddle'
6. Fasten the lid, turn on the 'Power Button', and select the 'ICE CREAM'' function.
7. Now, make a wide hole in the center that reaches the bottom of the pint.
8. Put the chopped roasted peanuts and mixed berries in the hole and select the "MIX-IN" function.
9. Dish out the ice cream from the pint and serve chilled.

Chocolate Brownie Ice Cream

Prep time: 5 minutes | Cook time: 3 minutes | Serves 4

- 1 tablespoon cream cheese, softened
- ⅓ cup granulated sugar
- 1 teaspoon vanilla extract
- 2 tablespoons cocoa powder
- 1 cup whole milk
- ¾ cup heavy cream
- 2 tablespoons mini chocolate chips
- 2 tablespoons brownie chunks

1. In a large microwave-safe bowl, add the cream cheese and microwave on High for about ten seconds.
2. Remove from the microwave and stir until smooth.
3. Add the sugar and almond extract and with a wire whisk, beat until the mixture looks like frosting.
4. Slowly add the milk and heavy cream and beat until well combined.
5. Transfer the mixture into an empty Ninja CREAMi pint container.
6. Cover the container with storage lid and freeze for 24 hours.
7. After 24 hours, remove the lid from container and arrange into the Outer Bowl of Ninja CREAMi.
8. Install the Creamerizer Paddle onto the lid of Outer Bowl.
9. Then rotate the lid clockwise to lock.
10. Press Power button to turn on the unit.
11. Then press Ice Cream button.
12. When the program is completed, with a spoon, create a 1½-inch wide hole in the center that reaches the bottom of the pint container.
13. Add the chocolate chunks and brownie pieces into the hole and press Mix-In button.
14. When the program is completed, turn the Outer Bowl and release it from the machine. 15. Transfer the ice cream into serving bowls and serve immediately.

Lite Chocolate Cookie Ice Cream

Prep time: 5 minutes | Cook time: 5 minutes | Serves 2

- 1 tablespoon cream cheese, at room temperature
- 2 tablespoons unsweetened cocoa powder
- ½ teaspoon stevia sweetener
- 3 tablespoons raw agave nectar
- 1 teaspoon vanilla extract
- ¾ cup heavy cream
- 1 cup whole milk
- ¼ cup crushed reduced-fat sugar cookies

1. Place the cream cheese in a large microwave-safe bowl and heat on high for 10 seconds.
2. Mix in the cocoa powder, stevia, agave, and vanilla. Microwave for 60 seconds more, or until the mixture resembles frosting.
3. Slowly whisk in the heavy cream and milk until the sugar has dissolved and the mixture is thoroughly mixed.
4. Pour the base into a clean CREAMi Pint. Place the storage lid on the container and freeze for 24 hours.
5. Remove the Pint from the freezer and take off the lid. Place the Pint in the outer bowl of your Ninja CREAMi, install the Creamerizer Paddle in the outer bowl lid, and lock the lid assembly onto the outer bowl. Place the bowl assembly on the motor base, and twist the handle to the right to raise the platform and lock it in place. Select the LITE ICE CREAM function.
6. Once the machine has finished processing, remove the lid. With a spoon, create a 1½-inch-wide hole that reaches the bottom of the Pint. During this process, it's okay if your treat goes above the max fill line. Add the crushed cookies to the hole in the Pint. Replace the Pint lid and select the MIX-IN function.
7. Once the machine has finished processing, remove the ice cream from the Pint.

Mint Cookies Ice Cream

Prep time: 5 minutes | Cook time: 3 minutes | Serves 4

- ¾ cup coconut cream
- ¼ cup monk fruit sweetener with Erythritol
- 2 tablespoons agave nectar
- ½ teaspoon mint extract
- 5-6 drops green food coloring
- 1 cup oat milk
- 3 chocolate sandwich cookies, quartered

1. In a large bowl, add the coconut cream and beat until smooth.
2. Add the sweetener, agave nectar, mint extract and food coloring and beat until sweetener is dissolved.
3. Add the oat milk and beat until well combined.
4. Transfer the mixture into an empty Ninja CREAMi pint container.

5. Cover the container with storage lid and freeze for 24 hours.
6. After 24 hours, remove the lid from container and arrange into the Outer Bowl of Ninja CREAMi.
7. Install the Creamerizer Paddle onto the lid of Outer Bowl.
8. Then rotate the lid clockwise to lock.
9. Press Power button to turn on the unit.
10. Then press Lite Ice Cream button.
11. When the program is completed, with a spoon, create a 1½-inch wide hole in the center that reaches the bottom of the pint container.
12. Add the cookie pieces into the hole and press Mix-In button.
13. When the program is completed, turn the Outer Bowl and release it from the machine.
14. Transfer the ice cream into serving bowls and serve immediately.

Vanilla Ice Cream With Chocolate Chips

Prep time: 5 minutes | Cook time: 5 minutes | Serves 4

- 1 tablespoon cream cheese, softened
- ⅓ cup granulated sugar
- 1 teaspoon vanilla extract
- ¾ cup heavy cream
- 1 cup whole milk
- ¼ cup mini chocolate chips, for mix-in

1. Microwave the cream cheese for 10 seconds in a large microwave-safe bowl. With a rubber spatula, blend in the sugar and vanilla extract until the mixture resembles frosting, about 60 seconds.
2. Slowly whisk in the heavy cream and milk until smooth and the sugar has dissolved.
3. Pour the base into an empty CREAMi Pint. Place the storage lid on the Pint and freeze for 24 hours.
4. Remove the Pint from the freezer and remove the lid from the Pint. Place the Pint in the outer bowl, install the Creamerizer Paddle onto the outer bowl lid, and lock the lid assembly on the outer bowl. Select ICE CREAM.
5. With a spoon, create a 1½-inch wide hole that reaches the bottom of the Pint. During this process, it's okay for your treat to press above the max fill line. Add chocolate chips to the hole in the Pint and process again using the MIX-IN program.
6. When processing is complete, remove the ice cream from the Pint.

Chapter 7
Smoothie Recipes and Beyond

Daiquiri Lime Soda Frozen Yogurt

- 1 quart container full-fat plain yogurt
- ¼ teaspoon salt
- 1 cup sugar
- 1/4 cup lime juice
- ¼ cup sprite
- 4 tablespoons rum

1. Place the yogurt in a bowl. Use a whisk to mix in the sugar and salt. Continue to whisk for about 4 minutes until the sugar dissolves. Then mix in the rum, and lime juice.
2. Pour the ingredients into your ice cream maker, and let it churn for 25 minutes.
3. Put the frozen yogurt in an airtight container and place in the freezer for at least 2 hours, until desired consistency is reached.

Divine Coffee Frozen Yogurt

- 1 quart container full-fat plain yogurt
- ¼ teaspoon salt
- 1 cup sugar
- 1 teaspoon vanilla extract
- 1 cup strong brewed coffee or espresso
- 1 tablespoon coffee grounds

1. Refer to note at the beginning of the chapter about freezing bowl.
2. Place the yogurt in a bowl. Use a whisk to mix in the sugar and salt. Continue to whisk for about 4 minutes until the sugar dissolves. Then mix in the vanilla extract, coffee, and coffee grounds.
3. Pour the ingredients into your ice cream maker, and let it churn for 25 minutes.
4. Put the frozen yogurt in an airtight container and place in the freezer for at least 2 hours, until desired consistency is reached.

Blackberry Sugar-free Keto Frozen Yogurt
Prep time: 5 minutes | Cook time:10 Minutes | Serves 10

- 4 cups blackberries
- 1 cup Greek yogurt
- 1 tablespoon lemon juice
- 1 teaspoon vanilla extract

1. Place all ingredients in a food processor. Pulse until smooth. Place in the fridge to chill.
2. Turn on the Cuisinart and pour in the mixture.
3. Churn for 10 minutes.
4. Transfer in an airtight container and freeze overnight.

Peanut Butter White Chocolate Soft Serve Ice Cream
Prep time: 5 minutes | Cook time:40 Minutes | Serves 6

- 2 cups heavy cream
- 1 cup milk
- 3⁄4 cup sugar
- 1 Tbs. vanilla extract
- 1/2 cup peanut butter slightly melted
- 2 ounces semi-sweet chocolate

1. Melt the chocolate in a medium sauce pan on low heat. Allow the chocolate to cool a bit.
2. While the chocolate is cooling, place the milk and cream in a bowl, and mix them together until well combined. Use a whisk to mix in the sugar. Continue to whisk for about 4 minutes until the sugar dissolves. Mix in the vanilla extract. Then whisk in the peanut butter, and then the chocolate.
3. Pour the ingredients into your ice cream maker, and let it churn for 25 minutes.

Fruity Coffee Smoothie Bowl

Prep time: 5 minutes | Cook time: 3 minutes | Serves 4

- 1 cup brewed coffee
- ½ cup oat milk
- 2 tablespoons almond butter
- 1 cup fresh raspberries
- 1 large banana, peeled and sliced

1. In a high-speed blender add all the ingredients and pulse until smooth.
2. Transfer the mixture into an empty Ninja CREAMi pint container.
3. Cover the container with the storage lid and freeze for 24 hours.
4. After 24 hours, remove the lid from container and arrange into the outer bowl of Ninja CREAMi.
5. Install the "Creamerizer Paddle" onto the lid of outer bowl.
6. Then rotate the lid clockwise to lock.
7. Press "Power" button to turn on the unit.
8. Then press "SMOOTHIE BOWL" button.
9. When the program is completed, turn the outer bowl and release it from the machine. 10. Transfer the smoothie into serving bowls and serve immediately.

Oat Banana Smoothie Bowl

Prep time: 10 minutes | Cook time: 5 minute | Serves 2

- ¼ cup quick oats
- ½ cup water
- 1 cup vanilla Greek yogurt
- 3 tablespoons honey
- ½ cup banana, peeled and sliced

1. Merge the water and oats and microwave for 1 minute on High.
2. Add the yogurt, banana and honey after removing from the microwave until well combined.
3. Move this mixture to the MAX FILL line of a CREAMi pint.
4. Fasten the lid of the pint and freeze for 24 hours.
5. After 24 hours, open the pint, fix it into the outer bowl of Ninja CREAMi along with the 'Creamerizer paddle'.
6. Fasten the lid, turn on the 'Power Button', and select the 'SMOOTHIE BOWL' function.
7. Dish out the smoothie from the pint and serve as desired.

Piña Colada Pops

Prep time: 5 minutes | Cook time: 5 minutes | Makes about 4 pops

- 1½ cups frozen pineapple chunks
- 1 cup coconut milk
- ½ cup pineapple juice

1. In a food processor or blender, combine the ingredients until smooth.
2. Spoon the mixture into molds, and add the sticks or tops.
3. Freeze for 6 hours, and enjoy.

Peaches Smoothie Bowl

Prep time: 10 minutes | Cook time: 5 minute | Serves 1

- 1 cup almond milk, unsweetened
- 1 cup ice
- 1 scoop vanilla protein
- ½ cup peaches, frozen
- 1 tablespoon chia seeds

1. In a blender, blitz all the ingredients until smooth.
2. Move this mixture to the MAX FILL line of a CREAMi pint.
3. Fasten the lid of the pint and freeze for 24 hours.
4. After 24 hours, open the pint, fix it into the outer bowl of Ninja CREAMi along with the 'Creamerizer paddle'.
5. Fasten the lid, turn on the 'Power Button', and select the 'SMOOTHIE BOWL' function.
6. Dish out the smoothie from the pint and serve as desired.

Pitaya Breakfast Smoothie Bowl

Prep time: 5 minutes | Cook time: 5 minutes| Serves 2

SMOOTHIE

- 1 cup frozen pitaya puree
- 1-2 bananas
- ½ cup frozen berries
- ½ cup almond milk
- 2 tablespoons vegetable protein powder

TOPPINGS

- 1 tablespoon hemp hearts
- 1 tablespoon bee pollen
- 2 tablespoons goji berries

1. Blend all smoothie ingredients together at medium speed, until a smooth puree forms.
2. Top with the delectable topping options and enjoy the scrumptious fare!

Fruity Coconut Smoothie Bowl

Prep time: 10 minutes | Cook time: 5 minute | Serves 2

- 1 cup coconut milk
- ½ cup berries, frozen
- 2 bananas, frozen
- 2 tablespoons sugar

1. Put all the ingredients into the MAX FILL line of a CREAMi pint.
2. Fasten the lid of the pint and freeze for 24 hours.
3. After 24 hours, open the pint, fix it into the outer bowl of Ninja CREAMi along with the 'Creamerizer paddle'.
4. Fasten the lid, turn on the 'Power Button', and select the 'SMOOTHIE BOWL' function.
5. Dish out the smoothie from the pint and serve as desired.

Pumpkin Pie Smoothie Bowl

Prep time: 5 minutes | Cook time: 5 minutes| Serves 2

SMOOTHIE

- ½ cup low-fat plain yogurt
- 1 cup milk
- 1 cup pumpkin puree
- 1 banana
- 1 tablespoon chia seeds
- 1 pinch ground ginger
- 1 pinch ground cinnamon
- 1 pinch ground cloves
- 1 pinch salt

TOPPINGS

1 tablespoon shredded coconut
1 granola bar, crumbled
2 whole wheat crackers, crumbled

1. Combine all smoothie ingredients in a blender, and pulse until smooth.
2. Pour into a bowl and sprinkle the toppings and a dollop of coconut cream on top, and dig in to the big bowl of heaven.

Berries Smoothie Bowl

Prep time: 5 minutes | Cook time: 5 minute | Serves 1

- 2 cups frozen berries
- ½ cup grapefruit juice
- 1 tablespoon sugar

1. In a large bowl, merge together the berries, grapefruit juice, and sugar.
2. Move this mixture to the MAX FILL line of a CREAMi pint.
3. Fasten the lid of the pint and freeze for 24 hours.
4. After 24 hours, open the pint, fix it into the outer bowl of Ninja CREAMi along with the 'Creamerizer paddle'.
5. Fasten the lid, turn on the 'Power Button', and select the 'SMOOTHIE BOWL' function.
6. Dish out the smoothie from the pint and serve as desired.

Green Matcha Mint Smoothie Bowl

Prep time: 5 minutes | Cook time: 5 minutes| Serves 2

- Smoothie
- 1/3 cup soaked raw cashews
- 3 cups loose-packed greens
- 3 bananas, frozen
- 3 sprigs of mint Leaves
- 3 teaspoon matcha powder
- 1 teaspoon vanilla powder
- 2 scoops vanilla protein powder
- 3 ½ cups unsweetened almond milk
- 1 tablespoon cacao nibs
- Maple syrup, to taste
- Toppings
- 1 tablespoon coconut flakes
- 1 tablespoon hemp seeds or sesame seeds
- 1 tablespoon cacao nibs
- 2 tablespoons puffed quinoa
- Few sprigs of mint

1. In an upright blender, blend all smoothie ingredients except cacao nibs, until a smooth consistency is achieved.
2. Toss the cacao nibs in the blender and pulse to break them up.
3. Pour into a bowl and shake up the smoothie with some of the topping assortments, and top it off with a dollop of whipped coconut cream.

Blueberry Buckwheat Smoothie Bowl

Prep time: 5 minutes | Cook time: 5 minutes| Serves 2

- Smoothie
- 1 cup buckwheat groats
- 2 cups blueberries
- 2 tablespoons maple syrup
- ½ cup milk
- 1 banana
- 1 teaspoon vanilla extract
- Juice of half a lemon

1. Soak buckwheat groats in water overnight and drain well in the morning.
2. Blend blueberries with maple syrup until a smooth puree forms.
3. Reserve half of this sauce and toss in the rest of the smoothie ingredients in the blender, until creamy.
4. Pour in a bowl, drizzle the remaining blueberry puree for a marbled effect and top with fresh fruits, as pleases your palette.

Rainbow Fruit Pops

Prep time: 5 minutes | Cook time: 5 minutes | Makes about 12 to 15 pops

- Red layer
  ½ frozen banana
  1 cup frozen strawberries
  ¼ cup frozen raspberries
- Water, to blend

- Orange layer
  ½ frozen banana
  ½ cup frozen mango
  Water, to blend

- Yellow layer
  1 frozen banana
  ½ cup frozen pineapple
  ¼ cup frozen peaches
- Water, to blend

- Green layer
  1 frozen banana
  ½ cup frozen pineapple
  1 large handful spinach
  Water, to blend

- Purple layer
- ½ frozen banana
  1 cup frozen blueberries
  ½ cup frozen cherries
  Water, to blend

1. In a food processor or blender, purée the red fruit layer and carefully spoon it into the molds. Repeat with all the other colors.
2. Add the sticks or tops.
3. Freeze for 6 hours, and enjoy.

Peaches And Cream Smoothie Bowl

Prep time: 5 minutes | Cook time: 3 minutes | Serves 4

- 1 can peaches in their juice
- ¼ cup vanilla yogurt
- 2 tablespoons agave nectar

1. Place the peaches in their juice, yogurt, and agave in a clean CREAMi Pint and stir to combine. Place the storage lid on the container and freeze for 24 hours.
2. Remove the pint from the freezer and take off the lid. Place the pint in the outer bowl of your Ninja CREAMi, install the Creamerizer Paddle in the outer bowl lid, and lock the lid assembly onto the outer bowl. Place the bowl assembly on the motor base, and twist the handle to the right to raise the platform and lock it in place. Select the Smoothie Bowl function.
3. Once the machine has finished processing, remove the smoothie bowl from the pint. Serve immediately with desired toppings.

Raspberry & Orange Smoothie Bowl

Prep time: 5 minutes | Cook time: 5 minutes | Serves 2

- 2 cups fresh raspberries
- ½ cup vanilla yogurt
- ¼ cup fresh orange juice
- 1 tablespoon honey

1. In an empty Ninja CREAMi pint container, place the raspberries and with the back of a spoon, firmly press the berries below the MAX FILL line.
2. Add the yogurt, orange juice and honey and stir to combine.
3. Cover the container with the storage lid and freeze for 24 hours.
4. After 24 hours, remove the lid from container and arrange into the outer bowl of Ninja CREAMi.
5. Install the "Creamerizer Paddle" onto the lid of outer bowl.
6. Then rotate the lid clockwise to lock.
7. Press "Power" button to turn on the unit. 8. Then press "SMOOTHIE BOWL" button.
8. When the program is completed, turn the outer bowl and release it from the machine. 10. Transfer the smoothie into serving bowls and serve immediately.

Oats and Banana Smoothie Bowl

Prep time: 10 minutes | Cook time: 5 minute | Serves 1

- ½ cup carrots, frozen
- 1 frozen banana, quartered
- ½ teaspoon cinnamon
- ¼ cup rolled oats
- 2 tablespoons vanilla Greek yogurt

1. Put the frozen carrots to the MAX FILL line of a CREAMi pint.
2. In a large bowl, merge together rolled oats, banana, vanilla Greek yogurt, and cinnamon.
3. Thoroughly blend and move the mixture in the CREAMi pint.
4. Fasten the lid of the pint and freeze for 24 hours.
5. After 24 hours, open the pint, fix it into the outer bowl of Ninja CREAMi along with the 'Creamerizer paddle'.
6. Fasten the lid, turn on the 'Power Button', and select the 'SMOOTHIE BOWL' function.
7. Dish out the smoothie from the pint and serve as desired.

Pumpkin Papaya Acai Breakfast Bowl

Prep time: 5 minutes | Cook time: 5 minutes| Serves 2

SMOOTHIE

- ½ can organic pumpkin puree
- ½ cup papaya
- 1 frozen unsweetened acai smoothie pack
- 1 ripe banana
- 1 tablespoon maca powder
- 1 tablespoon cinnamon and pumpkin spice
- 1 cup almond milk

TOPPINGS

- 1 tablespoon goji berries
- 1 tablespoon pomegranate seeds
- 1 banana, sliced
- 2 tablespoons cashews, roasted

1. Toss all smoothie ingredients in the blender and whip on high, until a smooth puree forms.
2. Top with your favorite crumbled granola bars, and turn your bowl in to a masterpiece with the rest of the topping ingredients.

Three Fruit Smoothie Bowl

Prep time: 5 minutes | Cook time: 3 minutes | Serves 2

- 1 cup frozen dragon fruit pieces
- ¾ cup fresh strawberries, hulled and quartered
- ¾ cup pineapple, cut in 1-inch pieces
- ½ cup low-fat plain yogurt
- 2 tablespoons agave nectar
- 1 tablespoon fresh lime juice

1. In a large high-speed blender, add all the ingredients and pulse until smooth.
2. Transfer the mixture into an empty Ninja CREAMi pint container.
3. Cover the container with the storage lid and freeze for 24 hours.
4. After 24 hours, remove the lid from container and arrange into the outer bowl of Ninja CREAMi.
5. Install the "Creamerizer Paddle" onto the lid of outer bowl.
6. Then rotate the lid clockwise to lock.
7. Press "Power" button to turn on the unit.
8. Then press "SMOOTHIE BOWL" button.
9. When the program is completed, turn the outer bowl and release it from the machine. 10. Transfer the smoothie into serving bowls and serve immediately.

Super Green Smoothie Bowl

Prep time: 5 minutes | Cook time: 5 minutes| Serves 2

SMOOTHIE

- ½ cup unsweetened coconut milk
- 2 tablespoons chia seeds
- ½ small avocado
- 2 cups frozen peaches
- 1 ripe banana
- Fresh ginger, 1" piece
- 2 pitted dates
- 1 cup spinach
- 1 teaspoon chlorella

TOPPINGS

- 1 tablespoon coconut flakes
- 1 pinch cinnamon
- 1 banana, sliced
- 1 tablespoon cacao nibs
- 2 tablespoons blueberries and raspberries
- 1 tablespoon hemp seeds

1. Blend all smoothie ingredients at high speed until smooth.
2. Transfer to a bowl and top with unsweetened coconut flakes, cinnamon, banana slices, cacao nibs, blueberries, raspberries and hemp seeds!

Fruity Crunch Smoothie Bowl

Prep time: 5 minutes | Cook time: 5 minutes| Serves 2

SMOOTHIE

- 1 cup chopped kale
- 1 tablespoon chia seeds
- 1 cup unsweetened almond milk
- 1½ cups mixed berries, preferably frozen
- 1 small banana, frozen
- 1-2 tablespoons agave

TOPPINGS

- 3 strawberries
- 1 tablespoon coconut shavings
- 1 granola bar, crumbled
- 1 tablespoon blueberries

1. Blend kale with almond milk and chia seeds, until a smooth puree forms.
2. Add the berries and bananas, taking pains to leave a little texture.
3. Pour the smoothie into a bowl and top with the scrumptious topping ingredients. Be creative with the presentation!

Raspberry Melon Baobab Smoothie

Prep time: 5 minutes | Cook time: 5 minutes| Serves 2

SMOOTHIE

- ½ cup frozen raspberries
- 1 cup frozen cantaloupe chunks
- 1 cup unsweetened almond milk
- 1 scoop vanilla protein powder
- 1 teaspoon baobab powder
- ½ teaspoon psyllium husks
- 2 tablespoons peanut butter (crunchy or smooth, optional)
- A few ice cubes

TOPPINGS

- 2 tablespoons blueberries
- 2 tablespoons toasted shredded coconut
- 1 tablespoon cacao nibs

1. Blend all the smoothie ingredients together, until a desired consistency is achieved.
2. Top with vibrant blueberries, coconut and cacao nibs and slurp. I mean eat!

Kiwi Pops

Prep time: 5 minutes | Cook time: 5 minutes | Makes about 6 pops

- 4 ripe kiwis, peeled
- 1½ cups pineapple juice
- 2 ripe kiwis, peeled and sliced

1. Combine the whole kiwis and the pineapple juice in a food processor just until combined. Do not overmix, or the seeds will taste bitter.
2. Pour a few tablespoons of the purée into each of your molds. Add a slice or two of kiwi fruit, and then finish filling the molds to the top.
3. Add sticks or lids.
4. Freeze for 6 hours, and enjoy.

Mixed Fruit Pops

Prep time: 5 minutes | Cook time: 5 minutes | Makes about 6 pops

- 1–2 ripe kiwis, peeled and sliced
  ½ cup blueberries
- 1 banana, sliced
- 1 peach, sliced
- 1–2 cups strawberries, sliced
- About 1 cup apple juice

1. Divide the fruit into the popsicle molds, alternating for variety.
2. Fill the molds with apple juice and add the sticks or tops.
3. Freeze for 6 hours, and enjoy.

Hibiscus Fruit Pops

Prep time: 5 minutes | Cook time: 5 minutes | Makes about 6 pops

- ½ cup water
- 2 tablespoons dried hibiscus flowers
- 1 (½- inch) piece ginger, grated
- 2 tablespoons chopped mint
  3 tablespoons honey
- 5 cups watermelon
- 1 tablespoon lemon

1. Combine all the ingredients in a blender or food processor, and mix until smooth.
2. Fill the molds and add the sticks or tops.
3. Freeze for 6 hours, and enjoy.

Peach & Grapefruit Smoothie Bowl

Prep time: 5 minutes | Cook time: 3 minutes | Serves 2

- 1 cup frozen peach pieces
- 1 cup vanilla Greek yogurt
- ¼ cup fresh grapefruit juice
- 2 tablespoons honey
- ¼ teaspoon vanilla extract
- ½ teaspoon ground cinnamon

1. In a high-speed blender, add all ingredients and pulse until smooth
2. Transfer the mixture into an empty Ninja CREAMi pint container.
3. Cover the container with the storage lid and freeze for 24 hours.
4. After 24 hours, remove the lid from container and arrange into the outer bowl of Ninja CREAMi.
5. Install the "Creamerizer Paddle" onto the lid of outer bowl.
6. Then rotate the lid clockwise to lock.
7. Press "Power" button to turn on the unit.
8. Then press "SMOOTHIE BOWL" button.
9. When the program is completed, turn the outer bowl and release it from the machine. 10. Transfer the smoothie into serving bowls and serve immediately.

Turmeric Avocado Banana Smoothie Bowl

Prep time: 5 minutes | Cook time: 5 minutes| Serves 2

SMOOTHIE

- 2 bananas, peeled and frozen
- 1 cup almond milk
- 2 tablespoons fresh turmeric
- ¼ ripe avocado
- 3 cups organic loose spinach
- 3 Medjool dates, pitted

TOPPINGS

- 1 tablespoon shredded coconut
- 2 tablespoon flax seeds
- 1 blood orange, thinly sliced
- 1 granola bar, crumbled

1. Toss all smoothie ingredients in to the blender and mix on high until the desired texture is achieved.
2. Top with shredded coconuts, Flax Seeds, blood oranges and Granola bars!

Kale VS Avocado Smoothie Bowl

Prep time: 5 minutes | Cook time: 3 minutes | Serves 4

- 1 banana, cut into 1-inch pieces
- ½ ripe avocado, cut into 1-inch pieces
- 1 cup packed kale leaves
- 1 cup green apple pieces
- ¼ cup unsweetened coconut milk
- 2 tablespoons agave nectar

1. Combine the banana, avocado, kale, apple, coconut milk, and agave in a blender. Blend on high for about 1 minute until smooth.
2. Pour the base into a clean CREAMi Pint. Place the storage lid on the container and freeze for 24 hours.
3. Remove the pint from the freezer and take off the lid. Place the pint in the outer bowl of your Ninja CREAMi, install the Creamerizer Paddle in the outer bowl lid, and lock the lid assembly onto the outer bowl. Place the bowl assembly on the motor base, and twist the handle to the right to raise the platform and lock it in place. Select the Smoothie Bowl function.
4. Once the machine has finished processing, remove the smoothie bowl from the pint. Serve immediately with your desired toppings.

Pumpkin & Banana Smoothie Bowl

Prep time: 5 minutes | Cook time: 3 minutes | Serves 2

- 1 cup canned pumpkin puree
- ⅓ cup plain Greek yogurt
- 1½ tablespoons maple syrup
- 1 teaspoon vanilla extract
- 1 teaspoon pumpkin pie spice
- 1 frozen banana, peeled and cut in ½-inch pieces

1. In an empty Ninja CREAMi pint container, add the pumpkin puree, yogurt, maple syrup, vanilla extract, and pumpkin pie spice and mix well.
2. Add the banana pieces and stir to combine.
3. Transfer the mixture into an empty Ninja CREAMi pint container.
4. Arrange the container into the outer bowl of Ninja CREAMi.
5. Install the "Creamerizer Paddle" onto the lid of outer bowl.
6. Then rotate the lid clockwise to lock.
7. Press "Power" button to turn on the unit.
8. Then press "SMOOTHIE BOWL" button.
9. When the program is completed, turn the outer bowl and release it from the machine. 10. Transfer the smoothie into serving bowls and serve immediately.

Dragon Fruit & Pineapple Smoothie Bowl

Prep time: 5 minutes | Cook time: 5 minutes | Serves 4

- 2 cups frozen dragon fruit chunks
- 2 cans pineapple juice

1. Place the dragon fruit chunks into an empty Ninja CREAMi pint container.
2. Top with pineapple juice and stir to combine.
3. Cover the container with storage lid and freeze for 24 hours.
4. After 24 hours, remove the lid from container and arrange into the Outer Bowl of Ninja CREAMi.
5. Install the Creamerizer Paddle onto the lid of Outer Bowl.
6. Then rotate the lid clockwise to lock.
7. Press Power button to turn on the unit.
8. Then press Smoothie Bowl button.
9. When the program is completed, turn the Outer Bowl and release it from the machine.
10. Transfer the smoothie into serving bowls and serve immediately.

Strawberry Mango Pops

Prep time: 5 minutes | Cook time: 5 minutes | Makes about 6 pops

- 3 cups mango purée
- 1 ½ cups strawberries, hulled and sliced
- 2 tablespoons honey

1. Stir the strawberries and honey into the mango purée.
2. Spoon the mixture into ice pop molds and add sticks or lids.
3. Freeze for 6 hours, and enjoy.

Peanut Butter Banana Pops

Prep time: 5 minutes | Cook time: 5 minutes | Makes about 6 pops

- 4 bananas, frozen
- ½ cup natural peanut butter
- 1 cup almond milk (unsweetened)
- 2 tablespoons maple syrup

1. In a food processor or blender, purée the ingredients together until smooth.
2. Add the sticks or tops.
3. Freeze for 6 hours, and enjoy.

Appendix 1 Measurement Conversion Chart

Volume Equivalents (Dry)

US STANDARD	METRIC (APPROXIMATE)
1/8 teaspoon	0.5 mL
1/4 teaspoon	1 mL
1/2 teaspoon	2 mL
3/4 teaspoon	4 mL
1 teaspoon	5 mL
1 tablespoon	15 mL
1/4 cup	59 mL
1/2 cup	118 mL
3/4 cup	177 mL
1 cup	235 mL
2 cups	475 mL
3 cups	700 mL
4 cups	1 L

Volume Equivalents (Liquid)

US STANDARD	US STANDARD (OUNCES)	METRIC (APPROXIMATE)
2 tablespoons	1 fl.oz.	30 mL
1/4 cup	2 fl.oz.	60 mL
1/2 cup	4 fl.oz.	120 mL
1 cup	8 fl.oz.	240 mL
1 1/2 cup	12 fl.oz.	355 mL
2 cups or 1 pint	16 fl.oz.	475 mL
4 cups or 1 quart	32 fl.oz.	1 L
1 gallon	128 fl.oz.	4 L

Temperatures Equivalents

FAHRENHEIT(F)	CELSIUS(C) APPROXIMATE)
225 °F	107 °C
250 °F	120 ° °C
275 °F	135 °C
300 °F	150 °C
325 °F	160 °C
350 °F	180 °C
375 °F	190 °C
400 °F	205 °C
425 °F	220 °C
450 °F	235 °C
475 °F	245 °C
500 °F	260 °C

Weight Equivalents

US STANDARD	METRIC (APPROXIMATE)
1 ounce	28 g
2 ounces	57 g
5 ounces	142 g
10 ounces	284 g
15 ounces	425 g
16 ounces (1 pound)	455 g
1.5 pounds	680 g
2 pounds	907 g

Appendix 2 The Dirty Dozen and Clean Fifteen

The Environmental Working Group (EWG) is a nonprofit, nonpartisan organization dedicated to protecting human health and the environment Its mission is to empower people to live healthier lives in a healthier environment. This organization publishes an annual list of the twelve kinds of produce, in sequence, that have the highest amount of pesticide residue-the Dirty Dozen-as well as a list of the fifteen kinds ofproduce that have the least amount of pesticide residue-the Clean Fifteen.

THE DIRTY DOZEN	
The 2016 Dirty Dozen includes the following produce. These are considered among the year's most important produce to buy organic:	
Strawberries	Spinach
Apples	Tomatoes
Nectarines	Bell peppers
Peaches	Cherry tomatoes
Celery	Cucumbers
Grapes	Kale/collard greens
Cherries	Hot peppers
The Dirty Dozen list contains two additional itemskale/collard greens and hot peppers-because they tend to contain trace levels of highly hazardous pesticides.	

THE CLEAN FIFTEEN	
The least critical to buy organically are the Clean Fifteen list. The following are on the 2016 list:	
Avocados	Papayas
Corn	Kiw
Pineapples	Eggplant
Cabbage	Honeydew
Sweet peas	Grapefruit
Onions	Cantaloupe
Asparagus	Cauliflower
Mangos	
Some of the sweet corn sold in the United States are made from genetically engineered (GE) seedstock. Buy organic varieties of these crops to avoid GE produce.	

Appendix 3 Index

NANNIE E. HORVATH

Printed in the USA
CPSIA information can be obtained
at www.ICGtesting.com
LVHW080210281123
765133LV00007B/60

9 781805 381358